FADE TO:

INT. PLUSH LIVING ROOM – NIGHT

GIANT TALKING CELERY IS RAPT WITH ATTENTION, NERVOUSLY TAPPING HIS PEN ON THE BACK OF HIS HEAD.

WELL, WHERE SHOULD I BEGIN? HOW FAR BACK SHOULD I GO? ALL THE WAY BACK TO WHEN I WAS JUST A SEEDLING ? ? ?

— Ronald Reagan
in TBD: The Movie
COMING SOON TO YOU AND ME

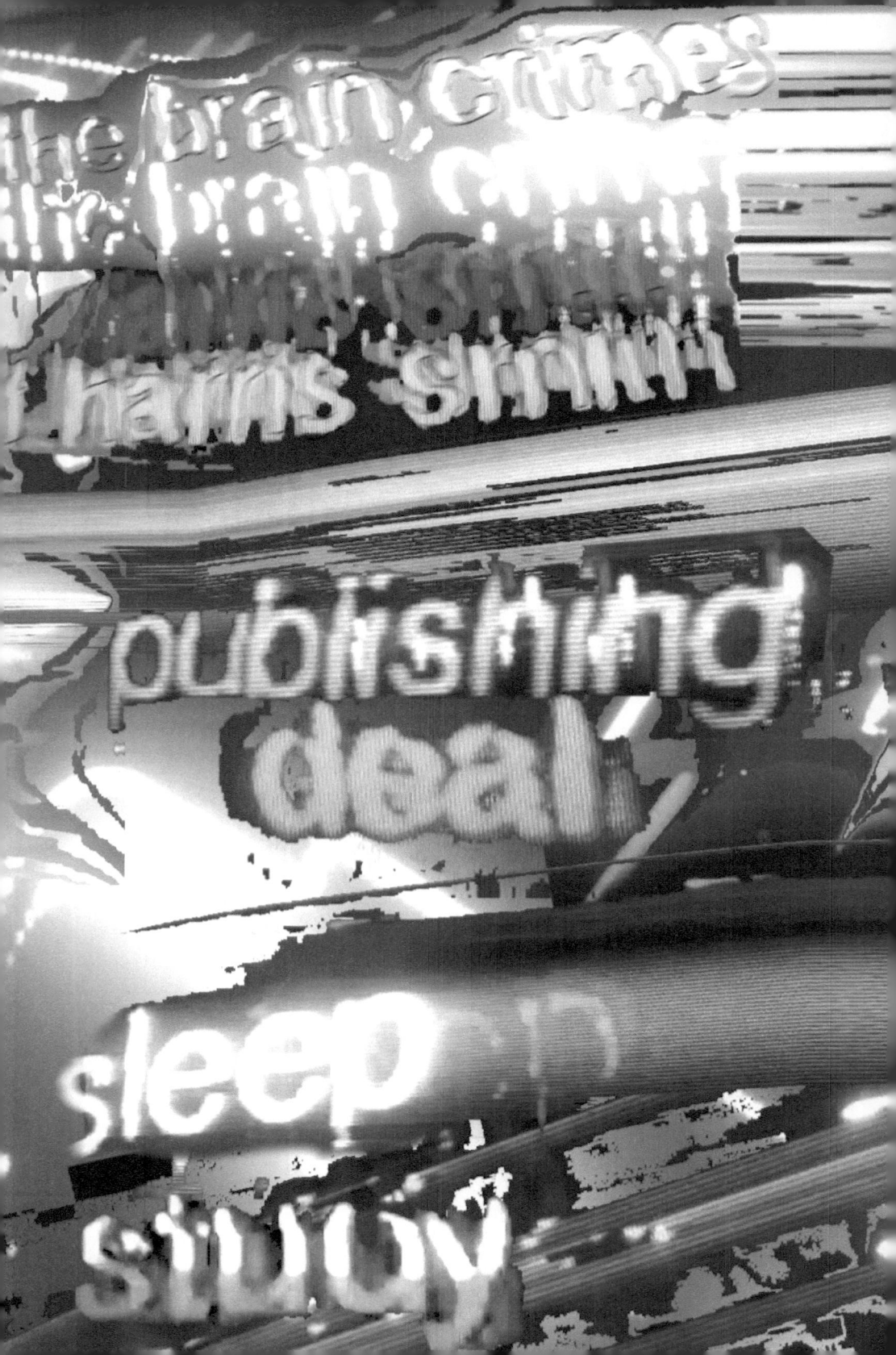

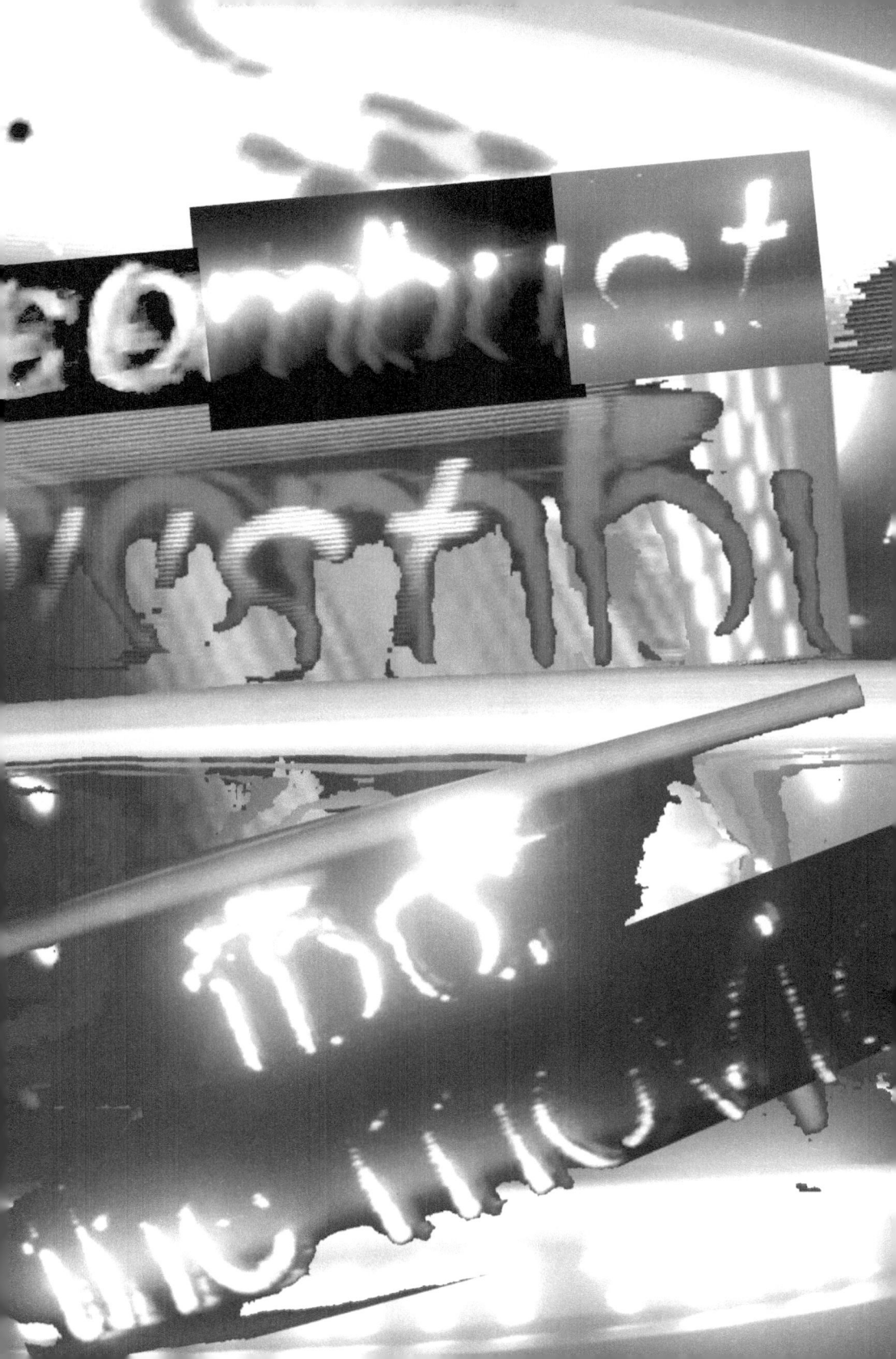

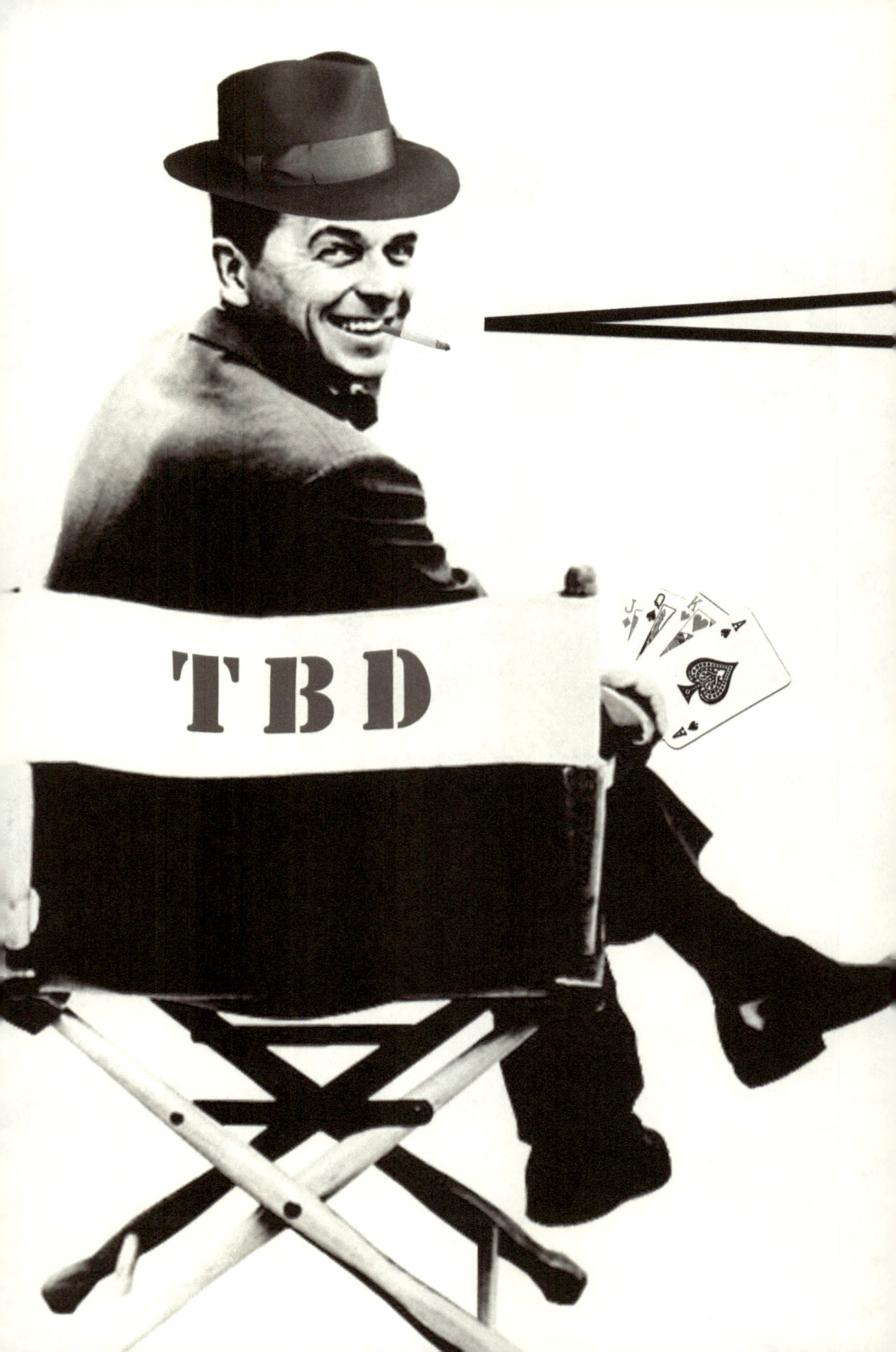

My fellow Americans...
Before I refuse to take
your questions I have an
opening statement. Thank
you on behalf of under
paid and underrepresented
arists everywhere. All of
the proceeds from TBD The
Zine will go to funding
TBD The Movie. The first
story on the list for TBD is
a story of crime and
punishment. One way to
make sure crime doesnt
pay would be to let the
government run it...

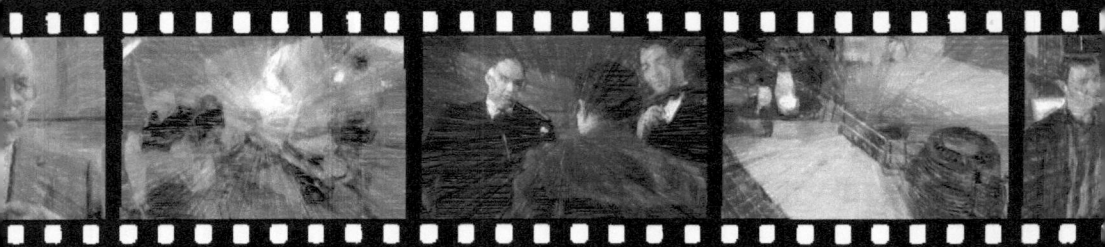

Publishing Deal

Written By Tom Garrett

Int. Film poster - day

A man sits on the floor
of a tiny, empty room.

His name is Ethan. He is
often very paranoid.

But this time, he knows
he only has 4 days
before he is killed.

Fade to black.

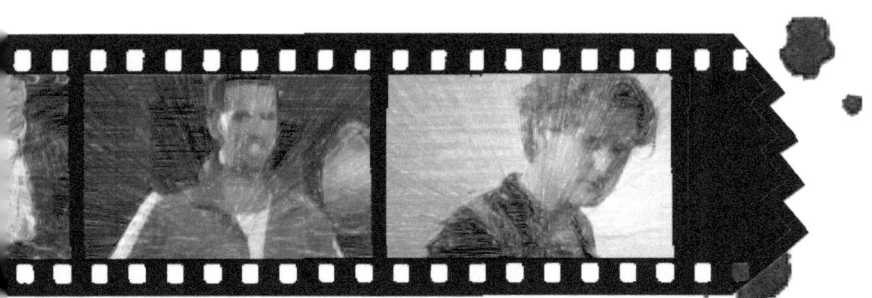

Ethan, a timid man of habit
with an affliction for science
fiction literature, finds
himself in a financially
crippling situation as he
scrambles to finish his novel.

Going to Big Donnie, the
ruthless, but not all too
dissimilar, head honcho of a
criminal syndicate, for money
could be his only way to get
the book finished.

Weeks later, Ethan sits with a
barely finished book and a
couple of crooks breathing
down his neck. Its due date,
and the pile of money is a lot
smaller than it should be.

tbd-movie.tumblr.com/pdeal

Written by Tom Garrett
mrtommygarrett.tumblr.com

Publishing Deal
(a cast of characters)

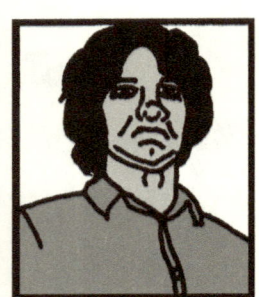

Ethan is a fragile man of habit. Always clean shaven, well groomed and smartly dressed (if not to stand out). He is Jewish, but only practices when around his family. His nervous disposition could be directly related to the guilt he feels towards the detachment he feels from his overbearing yet loving families beliefs, but he would never even come close to making such a connection. No, problems like this were better bottled up and thrown in a hole, "Happy thoughts, happy thoughts, happy thoughts…"

Over the years it built up, and the happy thoughts stopped coming. Slowly, over his 20's, Ethan began to detach from any confidence he had accumulated. A writer and lover of the arts is nothing with a fragile confidence. Dropped publishing deals and failed interviews leave him with nothing to call his own. "I might as well borrow a lump of money from Al Capone, that'll give me the kick up the butt I need to finish this damn thing," he would often think to himself when staring at his unfinished book, jokingly. A year or two later and he would rather forget that he was joking back then, as desperation has dragged him to such a situation. A suitcase of cash and a date to return it by, Ethan sets up shop in the cheapest place he can find in town. Finish the book, flee town or have a panic attack. This month would change his life.

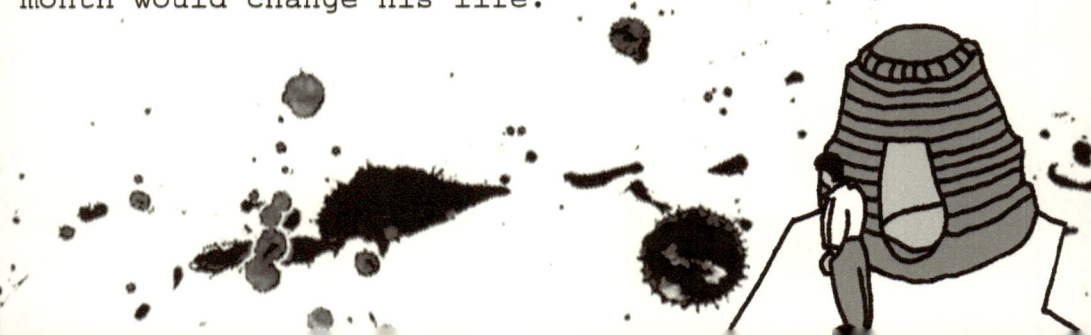

Publishing Deal
(a cast of characters)

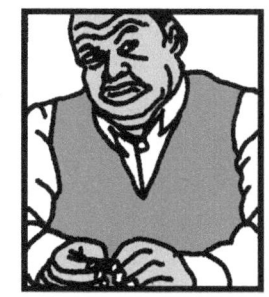

If you do *everything* as it comes, you do it *all*, right? **Donnie** had gotten by just fine by living by this rule. A simple, rational approach to things helped him get through school, past romances and conflicts. It had worked so well that he was almost beginning to consider himself some sort of genius. As opposed of course, to the large, slow kid at the back of the class he sometimes still saw in the mirror. He even knew, back then, that doing everything as it came to the best possible standard would get him far. Anyone that said he learnt that in special-ed class would get a brick in the face.

Donnie liked to get up at 10:05 every morning for eggs. It used to be eggs and bacon but its changed. Now it can be eggs and sausage, or toast. To Donnie, this was important. To Donnie most things were important. He had to play golf every saturday. He had to beat his personal best every two weeks. He even had a Wii installed in his office so he could practice when the boys were out. Getting better at golf was getting harder and harder, and knowing his perfectionist personality, he was starting to regret getting into it. His line of work didn't really bother him. It got him money and was one of the easiest ways of doing so, so there was no reason not to get into organised crime.

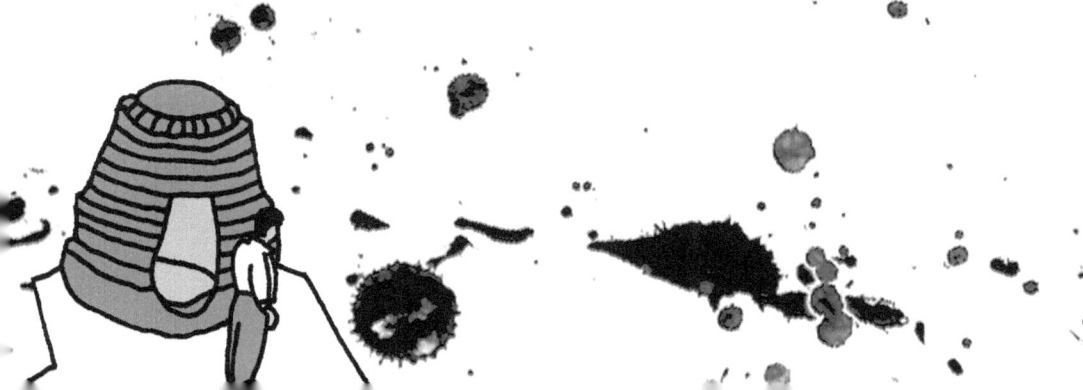

Publishing Deal
(a cast of characters)

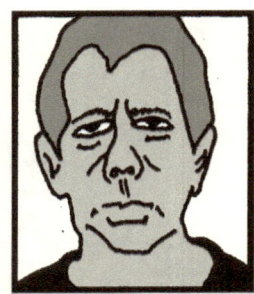

Malcolm was completely content with the position he found himself in. Good money, good fun, working for a big guy with a big agenda. He couldn't complain. He trusted in Donnie to take him places. He would follow his every word, because that was what brought the bread home. It was also usually a good laugh.

Malcolm found himself in this position for most of his life. In school he would always follow the tougher kids around, laughing at their jokes. This worked out fine for him. No need for thought intensive exercises. Why work more than you have to? He didn't consider it sucking up, he simply considered it the easiest way to have a comfortable life.

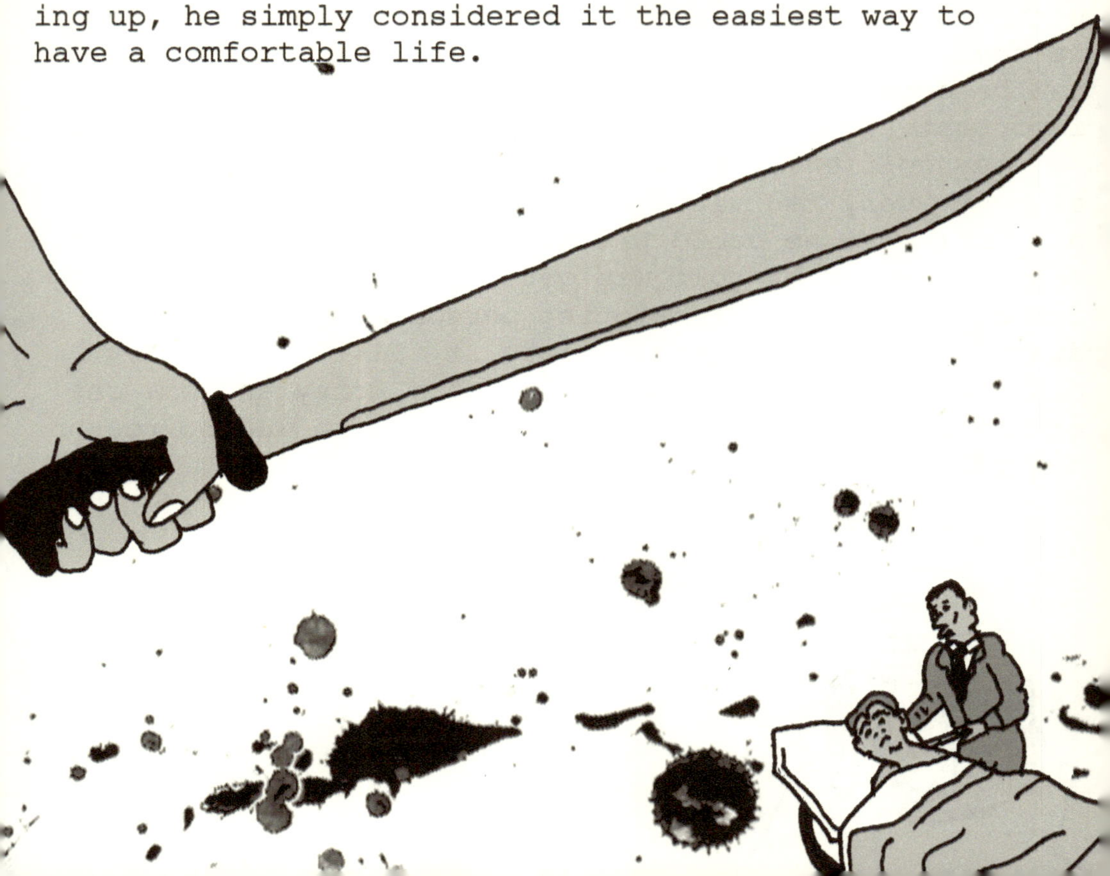

Publishing Deal
(a cast of characters)

John loved jazz. It was something about the rhythm and the warm twang of saxophone that would often times droop his eyelids and cause his hips to sway from side to side. Not that anyone knew that of course. Everyone saw him as the big guy. The bruiser. The one who you wanted on your side in a fight. Which was fine. He didn't need to really do anything but stand around and look scary, it was easy. There was no reason to pursue any other sort of life when pickings were this easy.

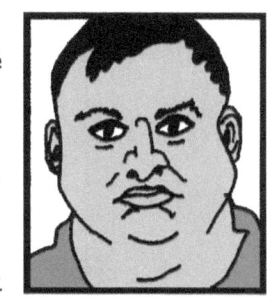

If only there was a way he could have musical hobbies alongside being hired muscle, but John couldn't find one. He was always scary looking, he figured, so that meant he was always on duty, which left no time to learn an instrument. He would often think about this, although it did make his head hurt…

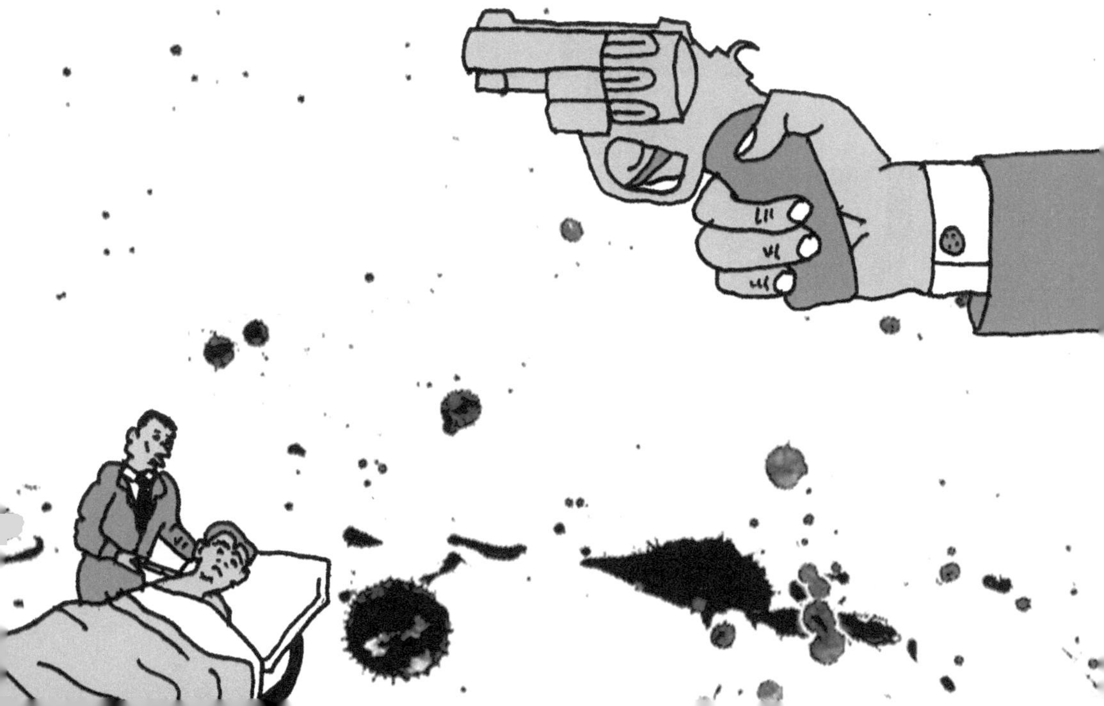

Publishing Deal Scene 1
Sample Storyboard

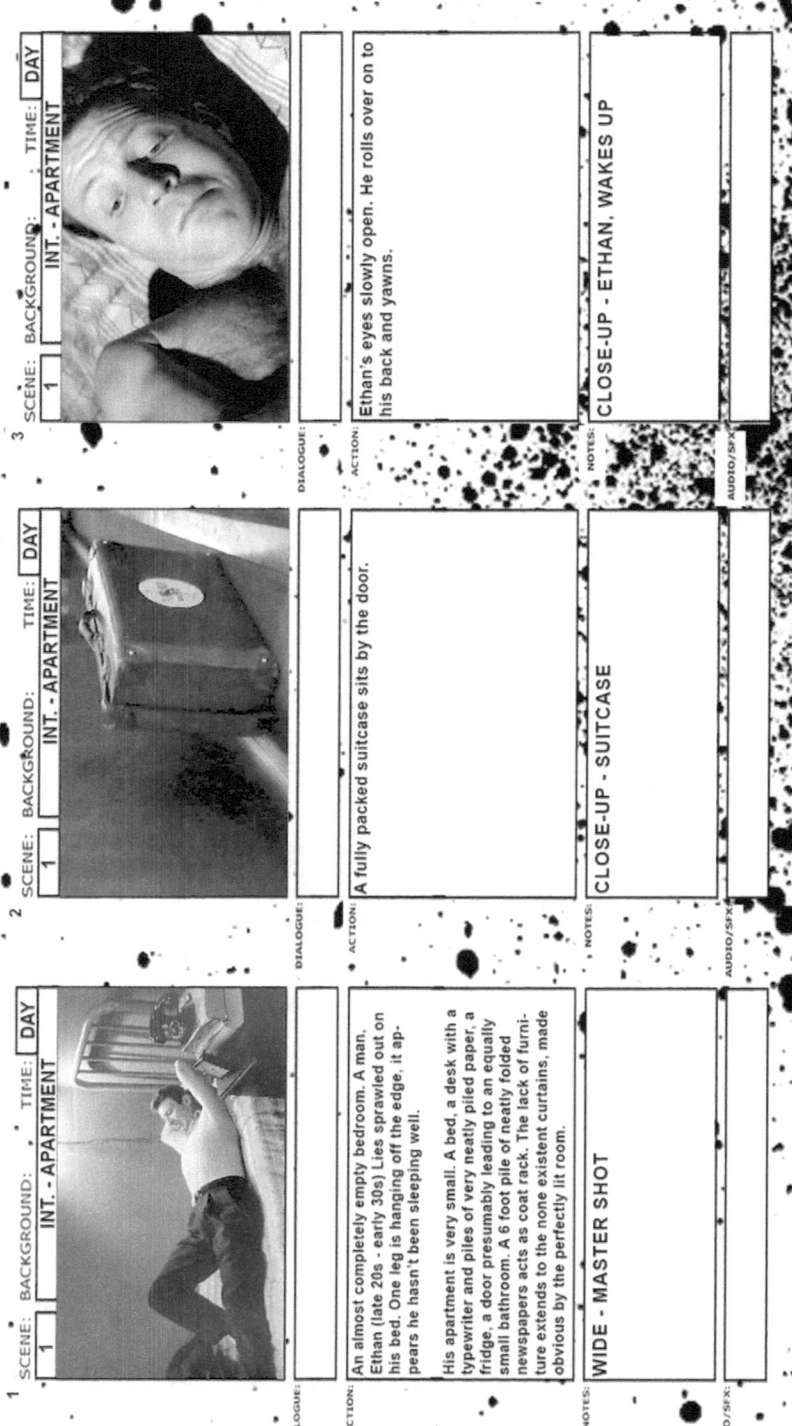

Panel 3

SCENE: 1
BACKGROUND: INT. - APARTMENT
TIME: DAY

DIALOGUE:

ACTION: Ethan's eyes slowly open. He rolls over on to his back and yawns.

NOTES: CLOSE-UP - ETHAN, WAKES UP

AUDIO/SFX:

Panel 2

SCENE: 1
BACKGROUND: INT. - APARTMENT
TIME: DAY

DIALOGUE:

ACTION: A fully packed suitcase sits by the door.

NOTES: CLOSE-UP - SUITCASE

AUDIO/SFX:

Panel 1

SCENE: 1
BACKGROUND: INT. - APARTMENT
TIME: DAY

DIALOGUE:

ACTION: An almost completely empty bedroom. A man, Ethan (late 20s - early 30s) Lies sprawled out on his bed. One leg is hanging off the edge, it appears he hasn't been sleeping well.

His apartment is very small. A bed, a desk with a typewriter and piles of very neatly piled paper, a fridge, a door presumably leading to an equally small bathroom. A 6 foot pile of neatly folded newspapers acts as coat rack. The lack of furniture extends to the none existent curtains, made obvious by the perfectly lit room.

NOTES: WIDE - MASTER SHOT

AUDIO/SFX:

Publishing Deal Scene 4
Sample Storyboard

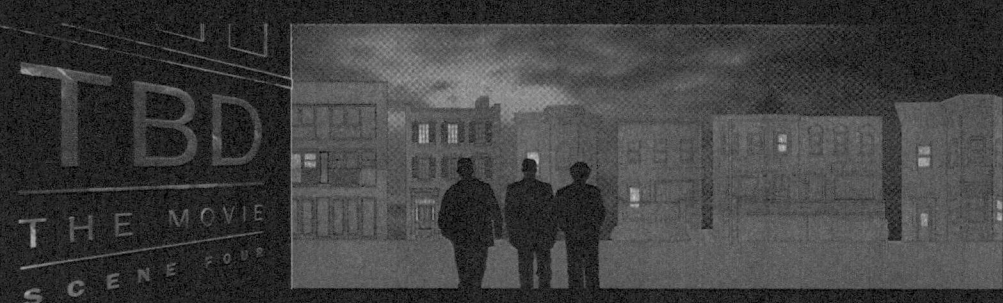

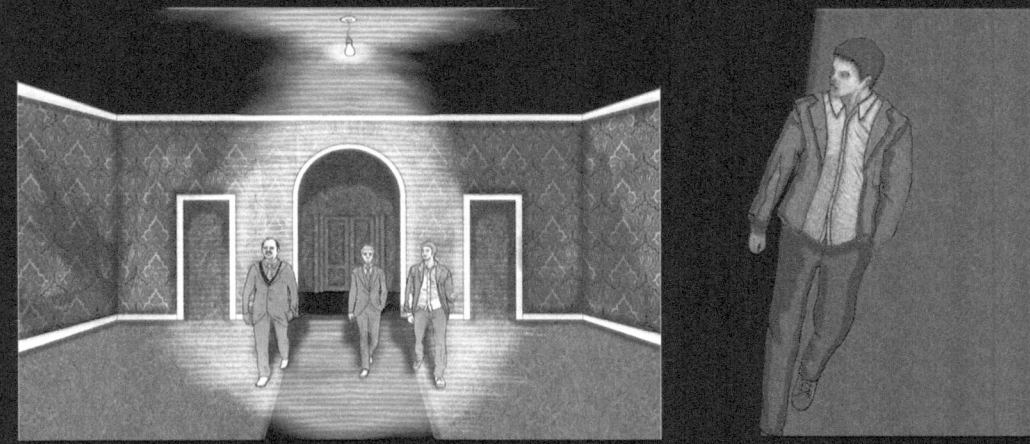

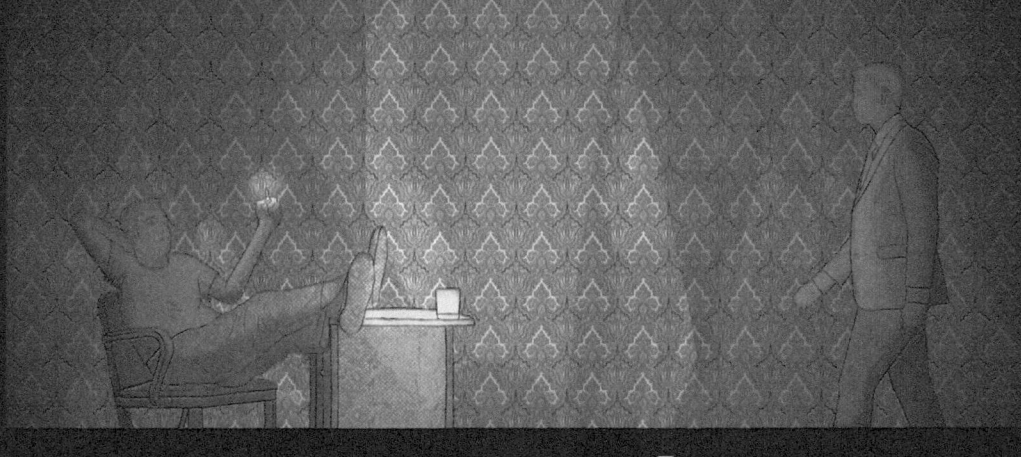

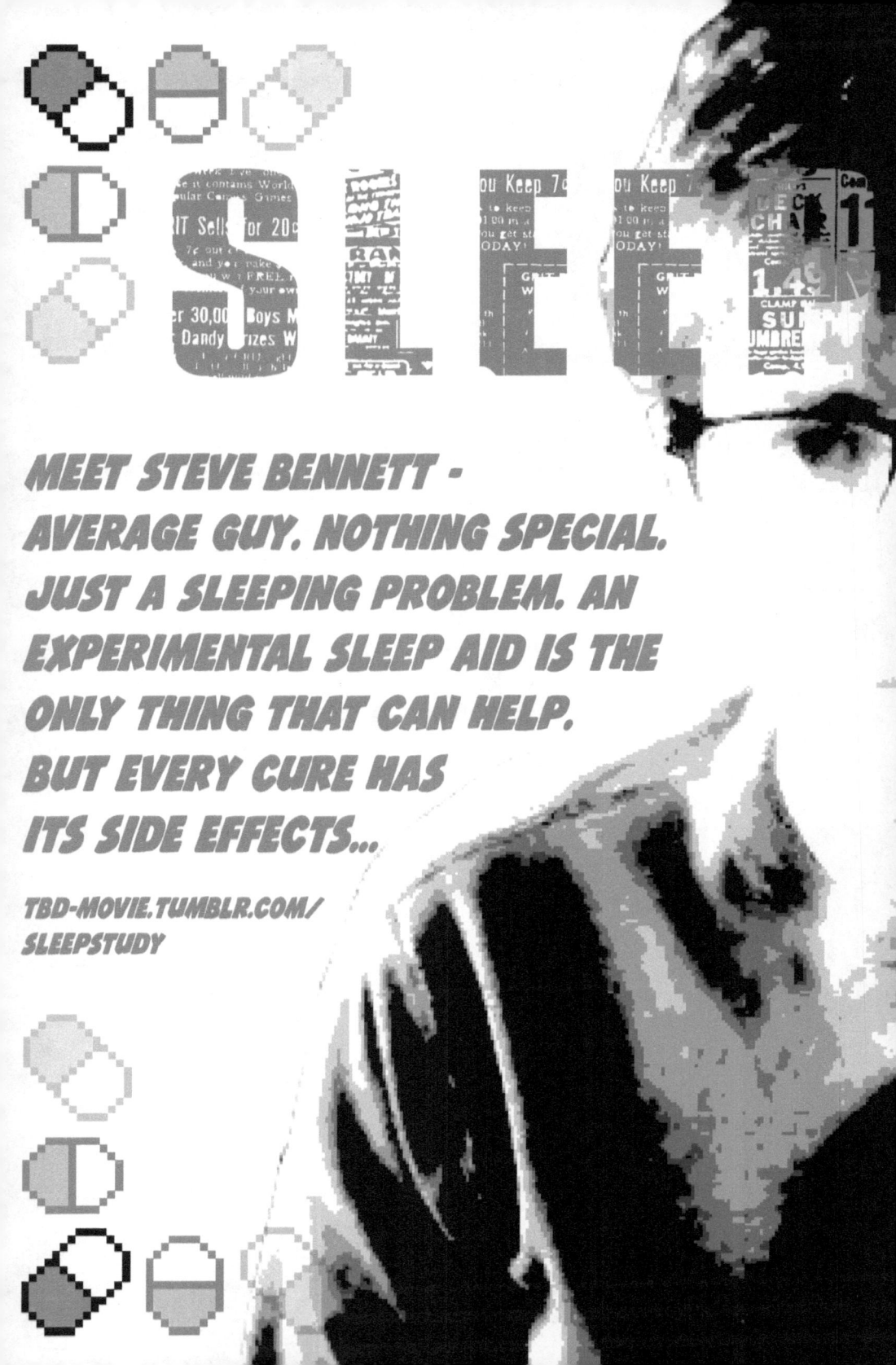

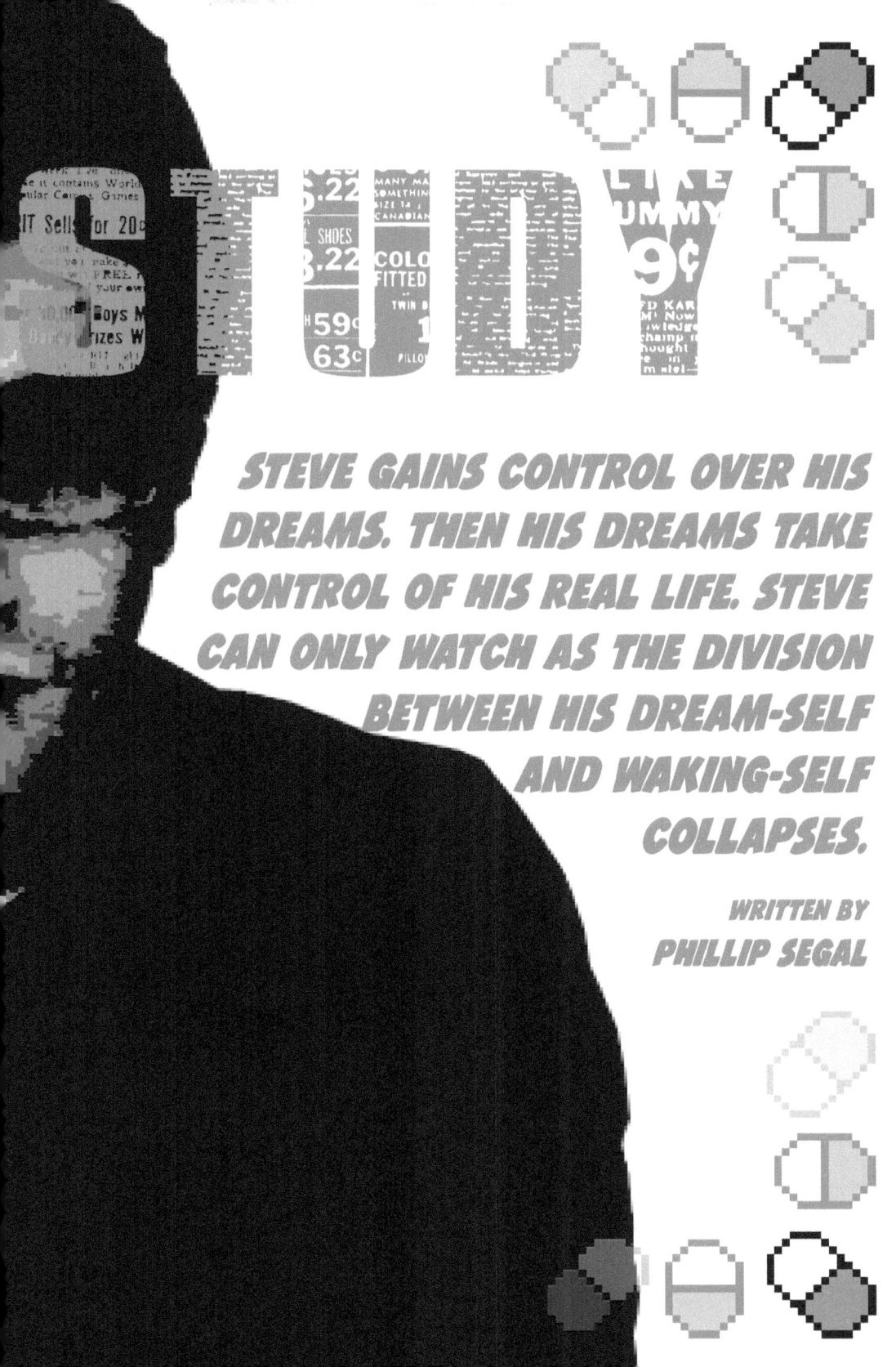

STUDY

STEVE GAINS CONTROL OVER HIS DREAMS. THEN HIS DREAMS TAKE CONTROL OF HIS REAL LIFE. STEVE CAN ONLY WATCH AS THE DIVISION BETWEEN HIS DREAM-SELF AND WAKING-SELF COLLAPSES.

WRITTEN BY
PHILLIP SEGAL

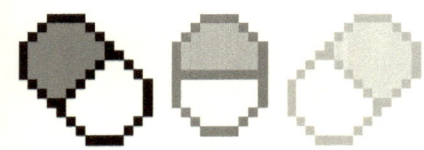

SLEEP STUDY
CHOOSE YOUR OWN ADVENTURE!

YOU FEEL EXHAUSTED. COMMUTING EVERY DAY HAS TAKEN ITS TOLL. YOU CAN'T STAND IT ANYMORE. YOU ARE SICK OF YOUR LIFE. YOU ARE SICK OF THE CUBICLE LIFE. YOU ARE SICK OF THE LIFE OF STEVE BENNETT.

MOST OF ALL, YOU ARE SICK OF NOT SLEEPING. YOU NEED TO SLEEP. EVERYBODY NEEDS TO SLEEP, BUT YOU REALLY, REALLY NEED TO SLEEP. IT HAS BEEN FAR TOO LONG SINCE YOU HAD A FULL NIGHT'S REST.

YOU PULL YOUR CAR INTO A DULL, GREY PARKING LOT. IT REMINDS YOU OF THE PARKING LOT AT WORK. IT ALSO REMINDS YOU OF THE PARKING LOT BACK HOME, BUT THIS AFTERNOON YOU'RE NOT AT WORK OR AT HOME. THIS AFTERNOON YOU'VE DECIDED TO TAKE ACTION.

YOU'VE TAKEN YOURSELF TO THE DOCTOR. YOUR VISITS WITH DR. PIBB HAVEN'T BEEN HELPFUL YET, BUT TODAY PROMISES TO BE DIFFERENT...

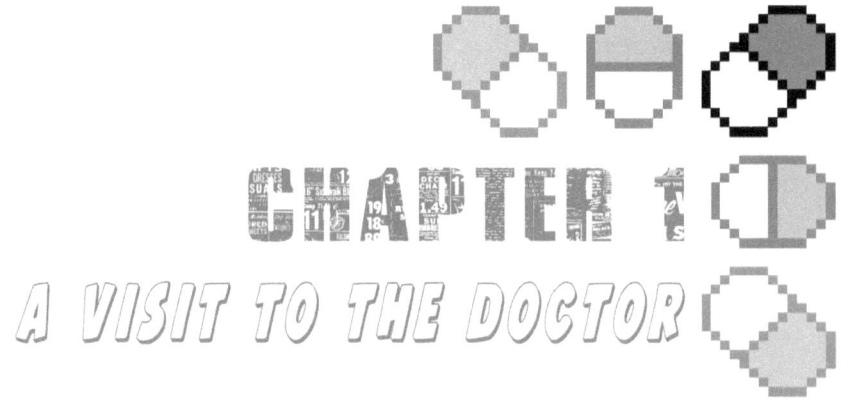

CHAPTER 1

A VISIT TO THE DOCTOR

A NURSE USHERS YOU IN TO DR. PIBB'S OFFICE. HE TELLS YOU ABOUT A NEW SLEEP AID BEING TESTED. HE THINKS IT MAY HELP YOUR CONDITION.

YOU QUICKLY AGREE TO THE TERMS. BEFORE YOU KNOW IT, YOU'RE ON YOUR WAY TO THE ADDRESS DR. PIBB GAVE YOU. IT IS A DULL, GREY TESTING FACILITY.

IT LOOKS A LOT LIKE YOUR DOCTOR'S OFFICE. THIS STARTS FEELING LIKE ANOTHER DEAD END, UNTIL YOU GET INSIDE. YOU CAN TELL THIS PLACE IS DIFFERENT. IT ACTUALLY FEELS WARM AND INVITING SOMEHOW.

THE DOCTOR LEADING THE STUDY TAKES YOUR APPLICATION AND SMILES AT YOU. "ARE YOU AWARE OF THE RISK INVOLVED, STEVE? ARE YOU SURE YOU STILL WANT TO DO THIS?"

GO TO PG. 20 IF YOU STILL WANT THE PILLS
GO TO PG. 22 IF YOU JUST WANT TO GO HOME

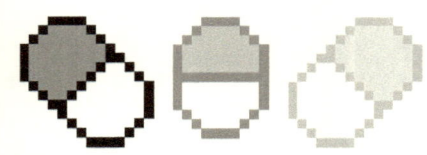

SLEEP STUDY
CHOOSE YOUR OWN ADVENTURE!

YOU ARE GETTING READY FOR BED BACK AT HOME. YOU TAKE A PILL, SWALLOW A GLASS OF WATER, AND LAY YOUR HEAD DOWN ON YOUR SOFT PILLOW. TONIGHT YOU DON'T THINK ABOUT WORK OR YOUR LIFE. YOU SLEEP.

YOU FIND YOURSELF STANDING ON A GRASSY HILL IN A COLD AND UNFAMILIAR COUNTRYSIDE. YOU HOLD AN ORNATELY CARVED BOX COVERED IN CRYPTIC DESIGNS THAT MAKE YOUR SKIN CRAWL.

YOU CAUTIOUSLY OPEN THE BOX AND DISCOVER A SILVER KEY - OBVIOUSLY FORGED BY THE SAME MASTER CRAFTSMAN WHO MADE THE BOX. YOU STRUGGLE TO UNDERSTAND THE MARKINGS COVERING BOTH. YOU FEEL THEY HAVE GREAT SIGNIFICANCE IN YOUR LIFE.

CLUTCHING THE KEY, YOU FEEL ITS WEIGHT PULL YOU UP THE HILL. YOU NOTICE A ROCKY OUTCROPPING AT THE TOP. THERE IS A SMALL CAVE ENTRANCE.

CHAPTER 2
THE DREAMQUEST BEGINS

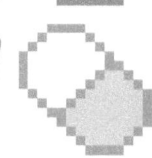

NORMALLY YOU WOULDN'T ENTER A MYSTERIOUS PORTAL TO THE UNDERWORLD, BUT YOU FEEL ENERGY PULSATING OUT OF THE KEY, GIVING YOU CONFIDENCE.

THE SMALL CAVERN QUICKLY GIVES WAY TO AN ENORMOUS CHAMBER DECORATED WITH OPULENT ATTENTION TO DETAIL. A MAN STANDS TO GREET YOU.

"HELLO STEVE, I AM RANDOLPH CARTER. GLAD TO MEET YOU... AGAIN. I SEE YOU FOUND THE KEY. REMEMBER, KEEP THE BOX WITH YOU AS WELL. YOU WILL NEED BOTH."

"I HOPE YOU FORGIVE ME FOR ASKING, STEVE, BUT I HAVE TO MAKE SURE. WHY ARE YOU ON YOUR JOURNEY? WHY AREN'T YOU SATISFIED WITH THE LIFE YOU HAVE?"

"I AM ON A QUEST TO UNLOCK THE DARK SECRETS OF THE UNIVERSE TO ATTAIN ULTIMATE POWER!" GO TO PG. 26
"I AM ON A QUEST OF UNDERSTANDING. I WISH TO KNOW MYSELF AND HELP MANKIND." GO TO PG. 28

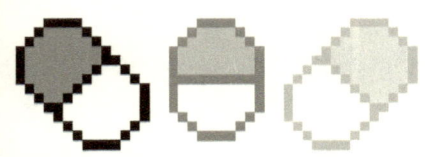

SLEEP STUDY

CHOOSE YOUR OWN ADVENTURE!

TURNING DOWN THOSE PILLS WAS PROBABLY THE BEST DECISION YOU'VE EVER MADE. YOU DON'T NEED SOME EXPERIMENTAL PHARMACEUTICALS MESSING WITH YOUR BRAIN CHEMISTRY. STILL, YOU CAN'T HELP BUT WONDER...

AFTER ANOTHER NIGHT OF RESTLESS TOSSING AND TURNING, YOU'RE BACK AT WORK. YOU STARE AT THE WALL OF YOUR DULL GREY CUBICLE AND IMAGINE WHAT IT WOULD FEEL LIKE TO BE SOMEONE ELSE. SOMETHING ELSE.

A COUPLE CUBICLE DWELLERS NEXT DOOR TO YOU ARE GRUNTING ABOUT THE BIG GAME AND TOSSING BACK A COUPLE BREWS. THEY WANDER OVER TO YOUR DESK AND ASK YOU IF YOU WANT TO JOIN THEM FOR A BEER AFTER WORK.

GO TO PG. 23 IF YOU LIKE THE SOUND OF THAT
GO TO PG. 24 IF YOU WOULD RATHER STAY AT HOME AND STARE AT A WALL THAN INTERACT WITH THESE IMBECILES

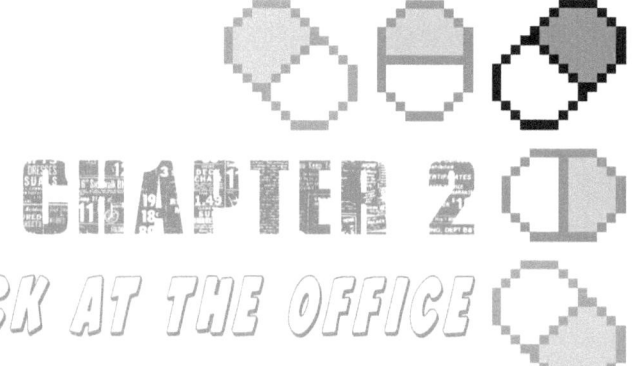

CHAPTER 2
BACK AT THE OFFICE

YOU GO OUT WITH "THE GUYS" AND GET SOME PITCHERS OF PILSNER AT THE LOCAL SPORTS BAR. SPORTS HAVE NEVER BEEN YOUR STRONG SUIT, BUT YOU PICK UP ENOUGH TO KEEP UP WITH THE GAME AND YOU HAVE FUN.

BEFORE LONG YOU'RE FITTING IN BETTER AT WORK AND GETTING ALONG WITH YOUR COWORKERS. YOU NO LONGER DREAD THE COMMUTE TO WORK. YOU ACTUALLY LOOK FORWARD TO IT. YOU EVEN START SLEEPING BETTER.

CONGRATULATIONS, YOU HAVE SUCCESSFULLY COMPLETED YOUR TRANSITION TO THE STATUS OF MEAT PUPPET. ENJOY YOUR MEANINGLESS EXISTENCE WITH THE REST OF THE WORKER DRONES.

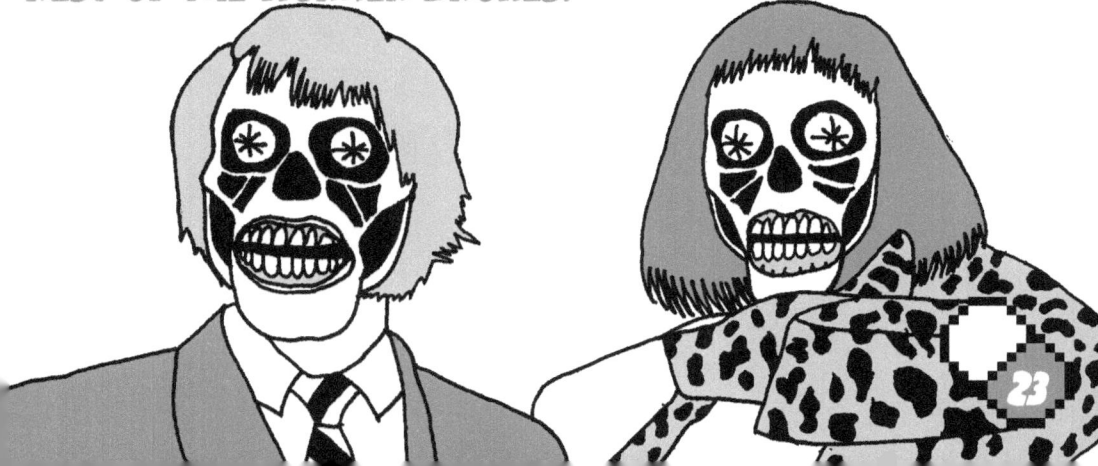

23

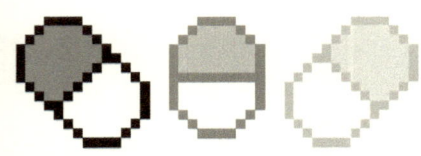

SLEEP STUDY
CHOOSE YOUR OWN ADVENTURE!

ALL WORK AND NO PLAY MAKES STEVE BENNETT A DULL BOY! THE DAILY GRIND EATS AT YOU FOR WEEKS, MONTHS, YEARS. YOU LOSE ALL DESIRE TO ENGAGE IN SOCIAL ACTIVITY. EVERYTHING BECOMES MEANINGLESS TO YOU. FOOD LOSES ITS FLAVOR.

YOU CAN'T STAND THE IDEA THAT NO ONE AT YOUR WORK FEELS THE WAY THAT YOU YOU DO. YOU NEED TO MAKE THEM SHARE YOUR PAIN.

YOU PARK YOUR CAR IN THE DULL, GREY PARKING LOT AT WORK ONE FINAL TIME. "THERE'S NO GOING BACK," YOU TELL YOURSELF.

YOU BURST INTO THE LOBBY WITH YOUR GUNS BLAZING. YOU ALWAYS WANTED TO BE RAMBO. NOW IS YOUR CHANCE. GIVE THEM HELL, STEVE!

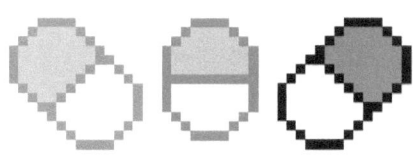

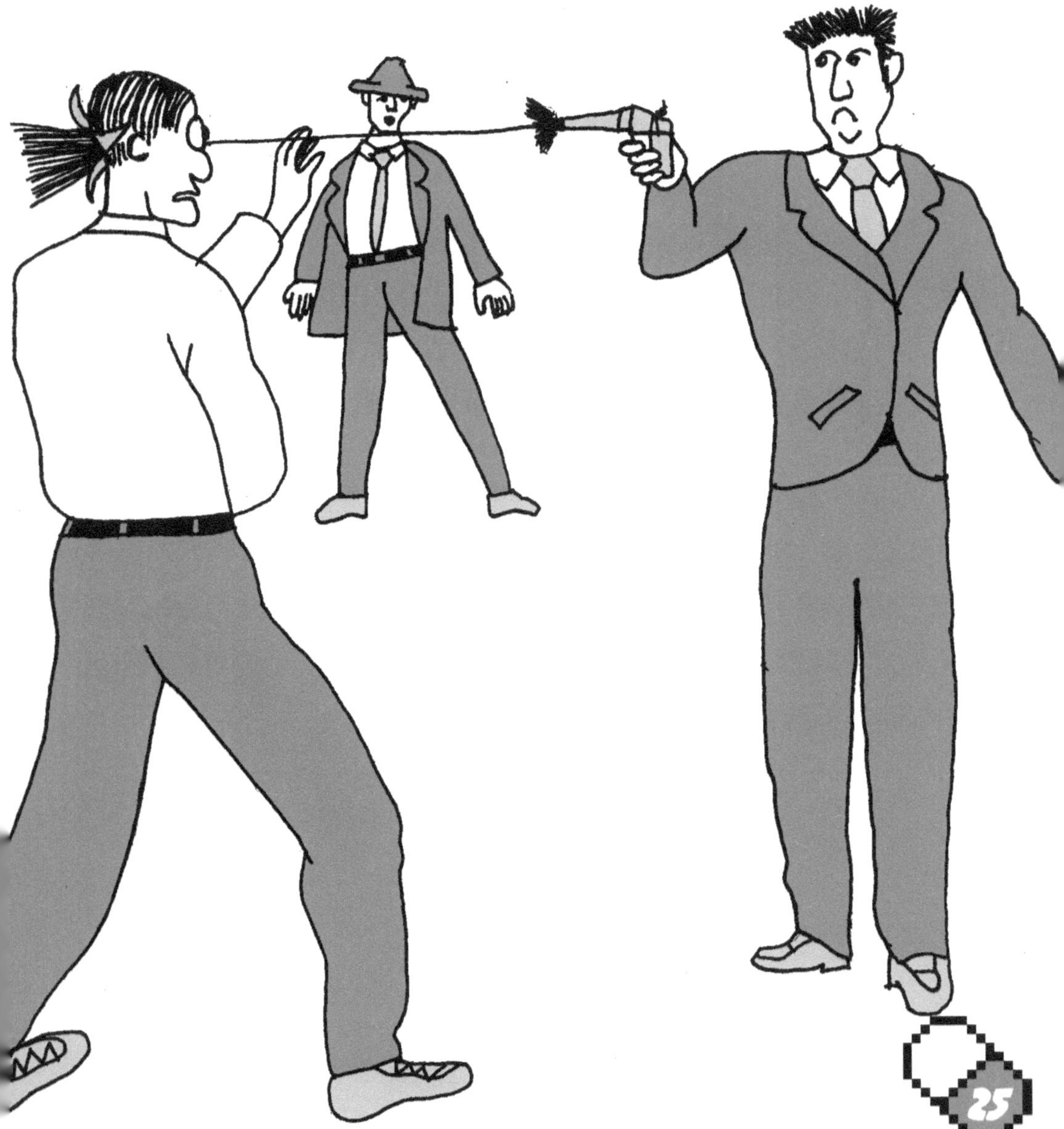

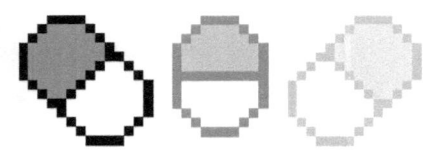

SLEEP STUDY

CHOOSE YOUR OWN ADVENTURE!

"VERY WELL," SAYS RANDOLPH CARTER, "IF YOU THINK YOU ARE PREPARED. HERE! THE LIMITLESS POWER OF THE UNIVERSE, AND IT'S ALL YOURS!"

YOU FEEL A SURGING RUSH OF WIND AND HEAT ENTERING EVERY ORIFICE OF YOUR HEAD. YOU HEAR THE CRACKLING OF ELECTRICITY AND SMELL SMOKE. YOU FEEL THE POWER OF THE UNIVERSE SURGING THROUGH YOU.

AN ENDLESS CORRIDOR OF LIGHT AND COLOR EXPANDS IN FRONT OF YOUR EYES. THE JOY AND TERROR OF CREATION FLOOD YOUR BRAIN. THE VISION EXPLODES INTO A CLOUD OF DEBRIS, AND A MOMENT LATER YOUR HEAD FOLLOWS WITH IT.

YOU ARE DEAD, STEVE. YOUR QUEST ENDS HERE.

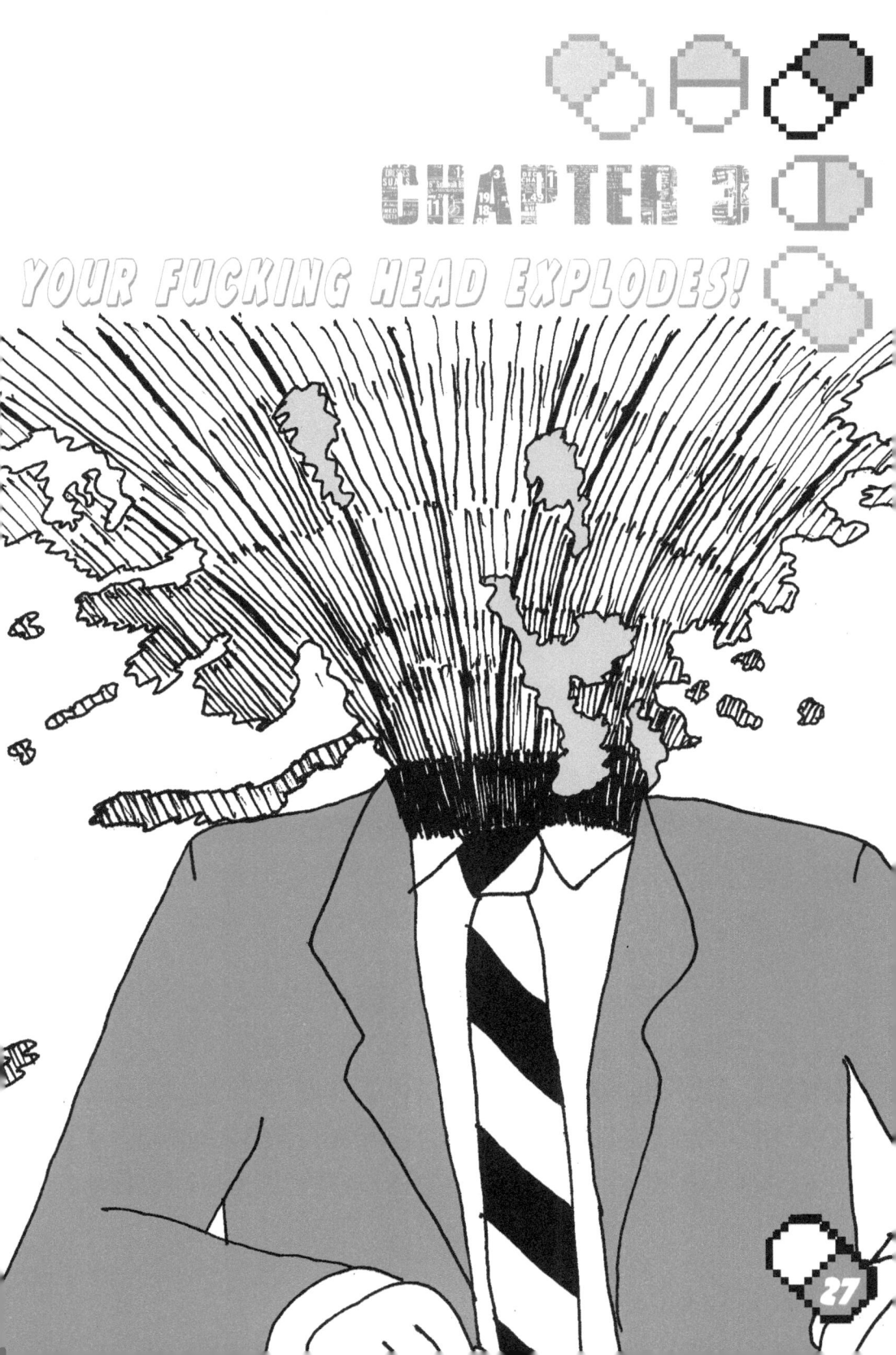

CHAPTER 3
YOUR FUCKING HEAD EXPLODES!

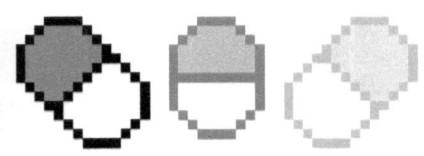

SLEEP STUDY

CHOOSE YOUR OWN ADVENTURE!

"YOUR INTENTIONS ARE HONORABLE," RANDOLPH CARTER SAYS. "TRY TO REMEMBER THEM WHEN YOU PASS THROUGH THE GATE."

BEFORE YOU CAN ASK ABOUT THE MEANING OF HIS WARNING, CARTER VANISHES INTO THIN AIR, TAKING THE ROOM WITH HIM. YOU FIND YOURSELF FLOATING IN A LIMITLESS BLACK EXPANSE.

AN IVORY PEDESTAL BECOMES VISIBLE FAR IN THE DISTANCE, AND YOU SEEM TO BE FLOATING TOWARD IT. AS YOU GET CLOSER, A SHAPE BEGINS TO FORM FLOATING OVER THE PEDESTAL. YOU TRY TO MAKE IT OUT.

THE SHAPE TAKES ON A FORM SIMILAR TO A MAN, BUT IT NEVER SEEMS TO SOLIDIFY. INSTEAD IT STAYS CLOUDY AND VAPOROUS, SHIFTING OUT OF FOCUS EACH TIME YOU FIX YOUR GAZE ON IT. SOMETHING MAKES YOU WANT TO TURN BACK, BUT YOU CONTINUE IN A TRANCE.

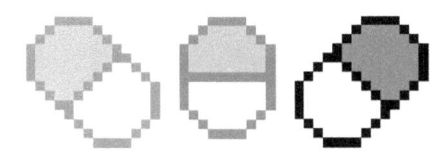

CHAPTER 3

THROUGH THE ULTIMATE GATE

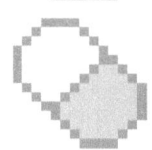

AS YOU NEAR THE PEDESTAL, THE SHAPE SPEAKS OUT TO YOU, BUT NOT IN ANY SOUND OR LANGUAGE. YOU CAN FEEL THE CREATURE TOUCHING YOUR MIND, MAKING YOU UNDERSTAND THINGS YOU'VE NEVER CONCEIVED OF.

YOU KNOW NOW THAT YOU ARE IN THE PRESENCE OF UMR AT-TAWIL, THE MOST ANCIENT ONE, WHO DWELLS AT THE OUTER BOUNDS OF DIMENSIONAL REALITY. YOU HAVE MADE IT TO THE GATE OF THE SILVER KEY.

UMR AT-TAWIL REACHES OUT TO YOUR MIND. "WELCOME STEVE BENNETT. THE ULTIMATE GATE IS READY FOR YOUR TRIAL, EVEN THOUGH YOU ARE LATE. IF YOU FEAR, YOU NEED NOT ADVANCE. WILL YOU ADVANCE?"

"I FEAR LOSING MY IDENTITY AND I WISH TO RETURN."
GO TO PG. 30
"I WILL ADVANCE AND I ACCEPT YOU AS MY GUIDE"
GO TO PG. 32

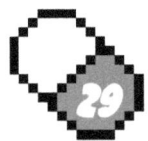

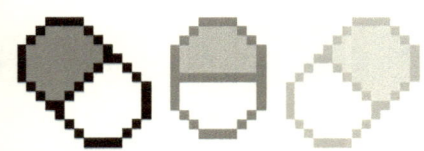

SLEEP STUDY

CHOOSE YOUR OWN ADVENTURE!

"YOU'VE GONE TOO FAR TO SIMPLY GO BACK NOW. DID YOU THINK I WOULD JUST SEND YOU BACK HOME?" UMR AT TAWIL'S WORDS RING THROUGH YOUR SKULL.

IN AN INSTANT YOU ARE ALONE AGAIN IN A LIMITLESS BLACK EXPANSE, THIS TIME YOU FEEL THAT YOU ARE FALLING. SOON THE FALLING SENSATION BECOMES MORE LIKE SINKING. THE COLD VOID BEGINS TO GET WARM AND YOU CAN FEEL SCRATCHING AGAINST YOUR SKIN.

SUDDENLY YOU CAN'T BREATHE, AND THE VOID AROUND YOU FILLS WITH HOT, GRITTY SAND. YOU THINK THIS CAN'T BE REAL. YOU THINK YOU'RE GOING TO SUFFOCATE. BEFORE ANY OF THESE THOUGHTS HAVE TIME TO GESTATE, YOU REALIZE YOU ARE NOT ALONE.

SOMETHING SLITHERS PAST YOUR LEG. YOU OPEN YOUR MOUTH TO SCREAM AND SWALLOW SAND. THEN A HUGE SANDWORM OPENS ITS MOUTH AND SWALLOWS YOU!

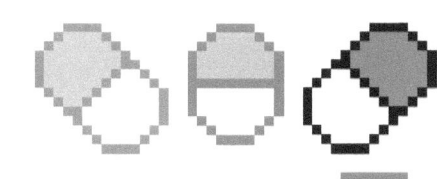

CHAPTER 4

IN THE BOWELS OF A SANDWORM

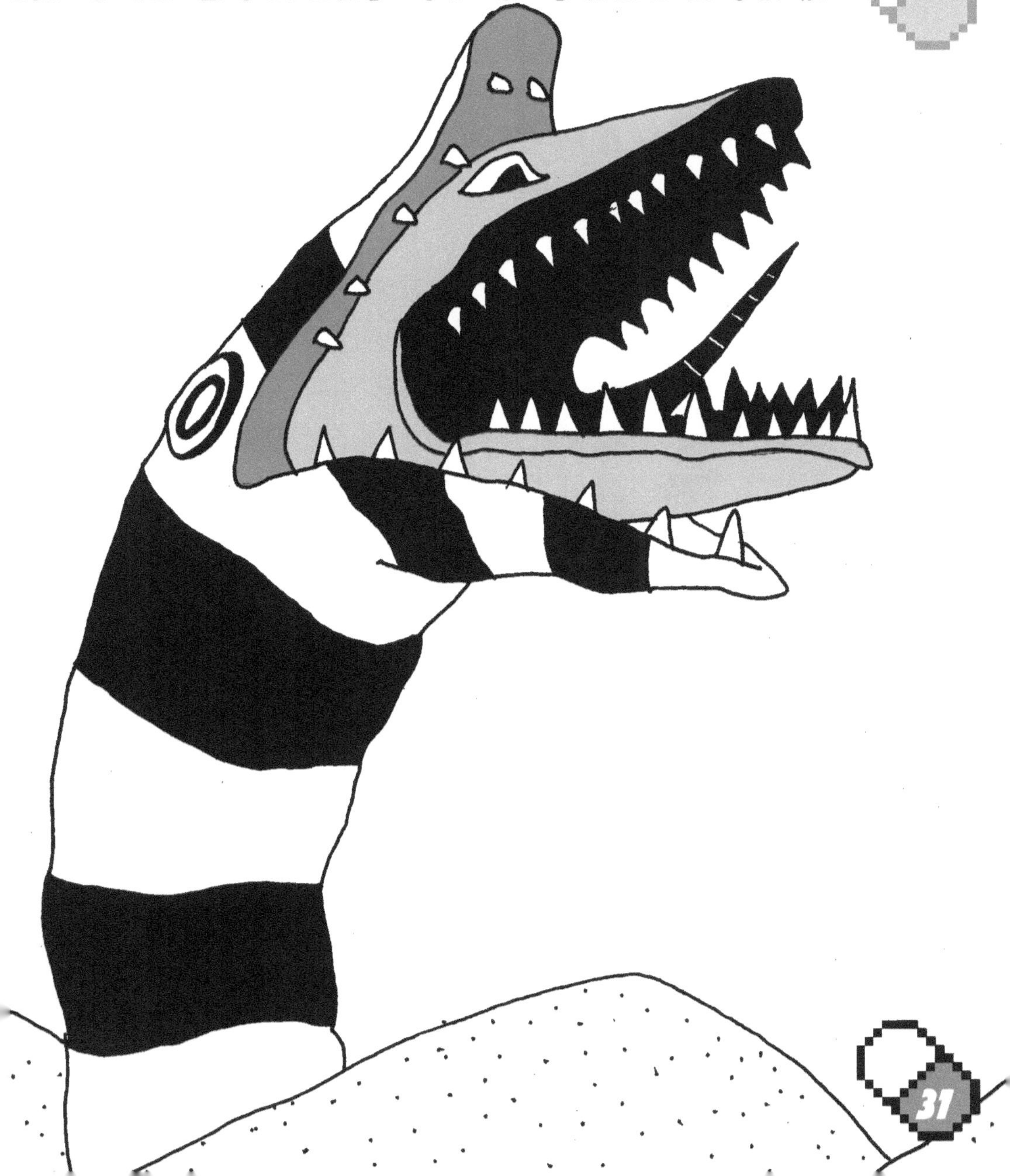

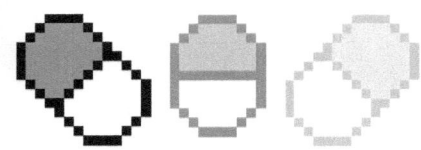

SLEEP STUDY

CHOOSE YOUR OWN ADVENTURE!

"ONE LAST THING BEFORE YOU CONTINUE," SAYS UMR AT-TAWIL. "THE MAN OF TRUTH IS BEYOND GOOD AND EVIL." WITH THOSE FINAL WORDS HE DISAPPEARS.

YOU BECOME DISORIENTED BY THE SUDDEN RETURN TO EMPTY DARKNESS. FOR THE FIRST TIME YOU FEEL HOW SHOCKING UTTER SILENCE, MENTAL AND PHYSICAL, CAN BE. YOU FEEL YOURSELF, STEVE BEENNETT, AS ONE FIXED POINT IN A COHESIVE DIMENSION.

THEN, ALL AT ONCE, AN EVEN GREATER SENSE OF TERROR BEGINS TO DISTURB YOUR SENSE OF UNITY. IN A MOMENT OF CONSUMING FRIGHT, YOU REALIZE THAT YOU ARE NOT ONE PERSON, BUT MANY PERSONS.

THERE ARE COUNTLESS STEVE BENNETTS LIVING THEIR LIVES AT DIFFERENT TIMES, IN DIFFERENT PLACES, ON DIFFERENT PLANETS, EVEN ON DIFFERENT DIMENSIONAL PLANES. THE STEVE BENNETT YOU KNOW IS A FRAGMENT.

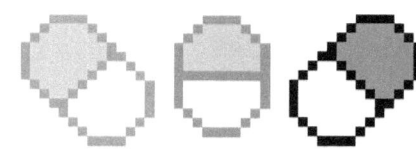

CHAPTER 4

AWAKENING OF INTELLIGENCE

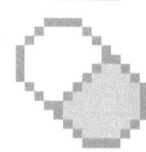

IN THE FACE OF THAT TERRIFIC REALIZATION, YOU FORGET THE HORROR OF YOUR OWN DESTROYED INDIVIDUALITY. YOU UNDERSTAND YOU ARE NOT MERELY A THING OF ONE SPACE-TIME CONTINUUM, BUT ALLIED TO THE ULTIMATE ANIMATING ESSENCE OF EXISTENCE'S SWEEP.

YOU BECOME VAGUELY AWARE THAT YOU ARE STILL HOLDING THE KEY AND ITS BOX. YOU READ THE SYMBOLS ON EACH THAT ONCE SEEMED SO STRANGE, AND THEY NOW MAKE PERFECT SENSE TO YOU.

YOU UNDERSTAND THAT THE BOX IS A CIPHER. THE KEY HOLDS THE CODE, WHICH WORK TOGETHER LIKE A QUESTION AND AN ANSWER. WHEN COMBINED THEY LEAD YOU TO THE ULTIMATE DISCOVERY.

STEVE BENNETT IS MERELY ONE OF THE INFINITE PHASES OF THE ARCHETYPAL AND ETERNAL BEING IN THE SPACE OUTSIDE OF DIMENSIONS. ARMED WITH THIS NEW KNOWLEDGE, YOU CAN NOW SAVE HUMANITY!

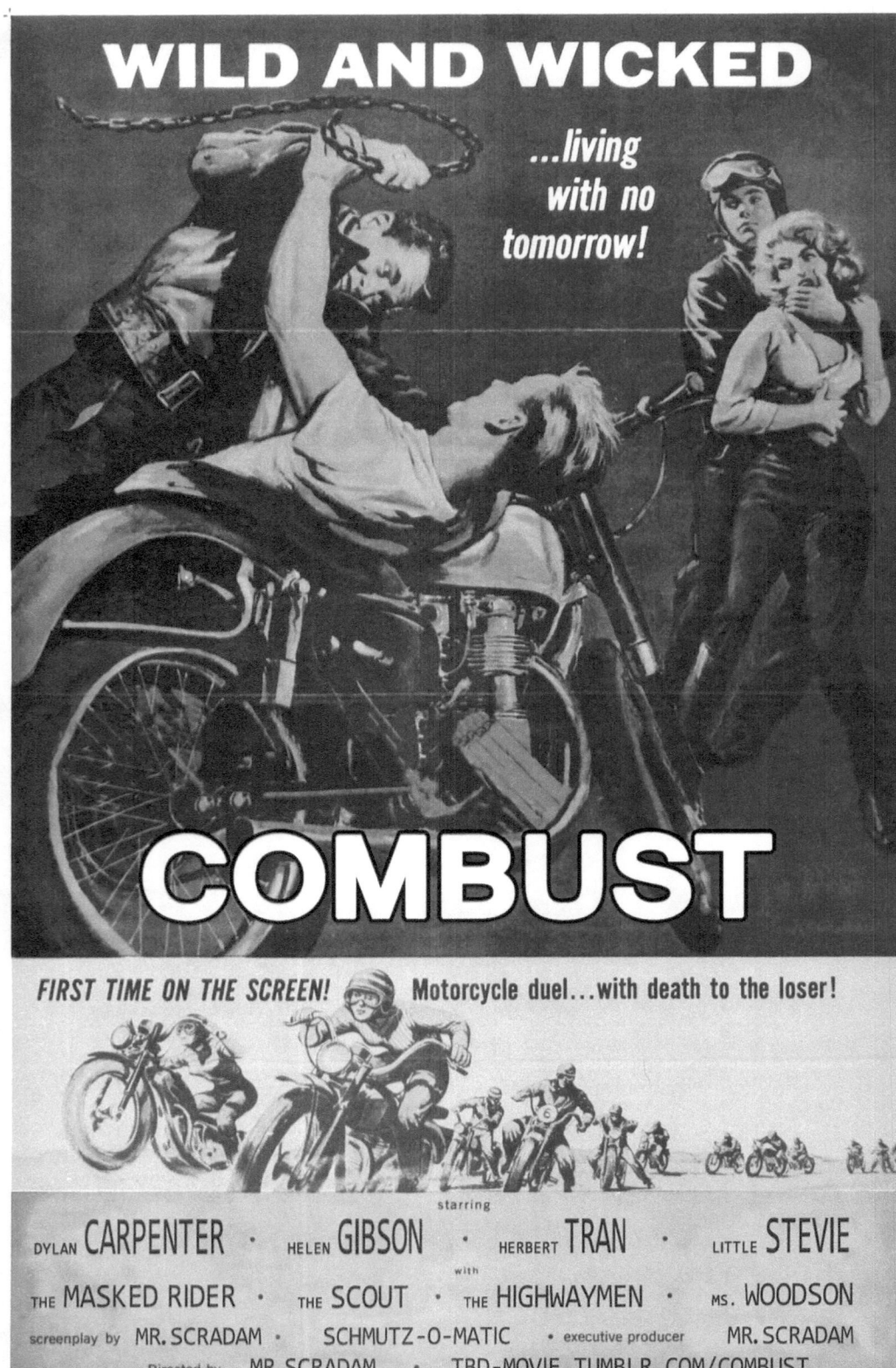

A KID AND HIS CAR
A WOMAN AND HER MOTORCYCLE
A BIKER GANG ON A HUNT FOR <u>HUMAN</u> FLESH!
WATCH WHAT HAPPENS WHEN THEY...

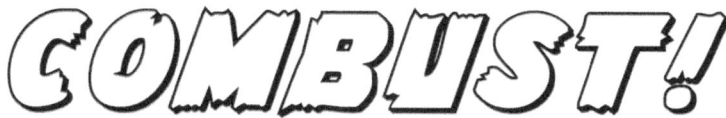

COMBUST!

DYLAN NEVER FIT IN AT HOME, AT "THE COLONY". EVERYONE WAS ALWAYS TOO CONCERNED WITH TENDING THE FIELDS AND RAISING FAMILIES. HE JUST WANTED TO BE LEFT ALONE IN HIS GARAGE WITH HIS TOOLS AND HIS DREAM CAR: AN ACCURATELY RECREATED VW BEETLE, COMPLETE WITH A VINTAGE COMBUSTION ENGINE.

THAT WAS BEFORE HE GOT OUT ON THE ROAD AND SAW WHAT THE WORLD HAD LEFT TO OFFER. SURE, THERE WERE MORE WOMEN HIS AGE OUTSIDE OF THE COLONY. BUT THERE WERE ALSO MORE PEOPLE WHO WANTED TO KILL HIM AND EAT HIM FOR DINNER.

NOW IT SEEMS LIKE THE COLONY WASN'T SUCH A BAD PLACE TO GROW UP AFTER ALL. EXCEPT FOR THE LACK OF WOMEN, THAT IS.

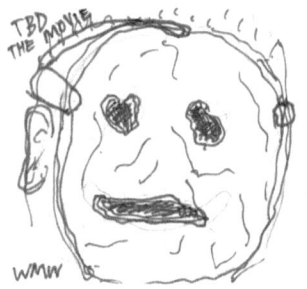

WRITTEN BY MR. SCRADAM
AND SCHMUTZ-O-MATIC

TBD-MOVIE.TUMBLR.COM/COMBUST

TBD: The Gathering

-PRESENTS-

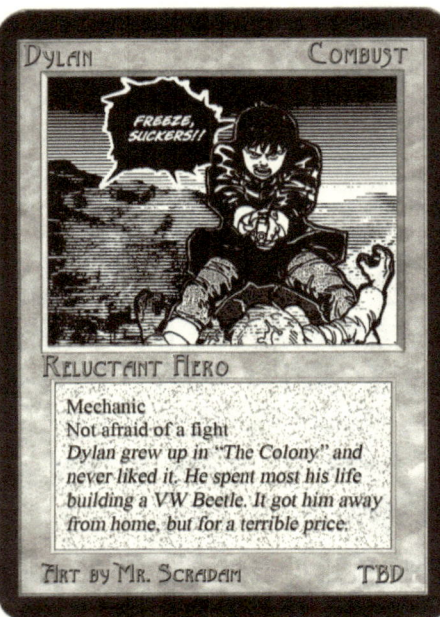

Dylan — COMBUST

RELUCTANT HERO

Mechanic
Not afraid of a fight
Dylan grew up in "The Colony" and never liked it. He spent most his life building a VW Beetle. It got him away from home, but for a terrible price.

Art by Mr. Scradam — TBD

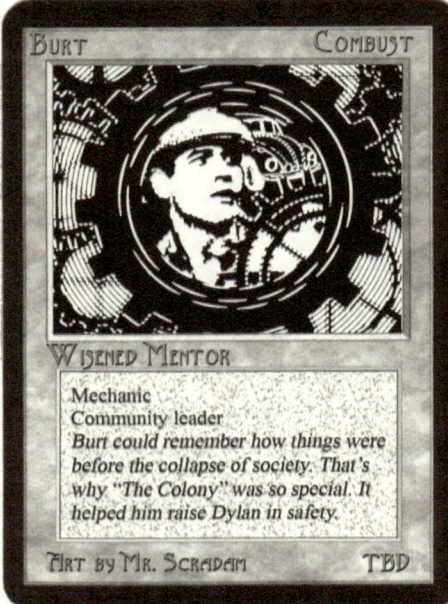

Burt — COMBUST

WISENED MENTOR

Mechanic
Community leader
Burt could remember how things were before the collapse of society. That's why "The Colony" was so special. It helped him raise Dylan in safety.

Art by Mr. Scradam — TBD

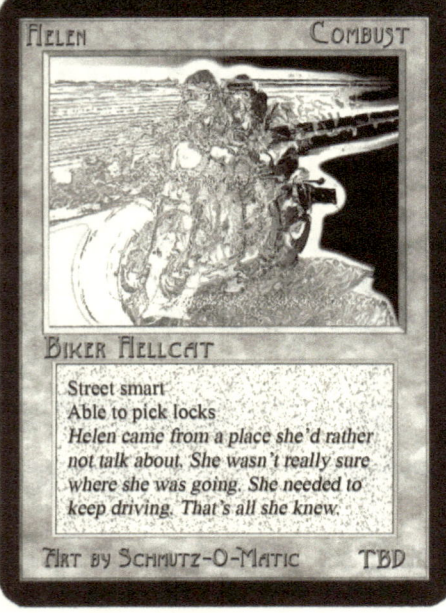

Helen — COMBUST

BIKER HELLCAT

Street smart
Able to pick locks
Helen came from a place she'd rather not talk about. She wasn't really sure where she was going. She needed to keep driving. That's all she knew.

Art by Schmutz-O-Matic — TBD

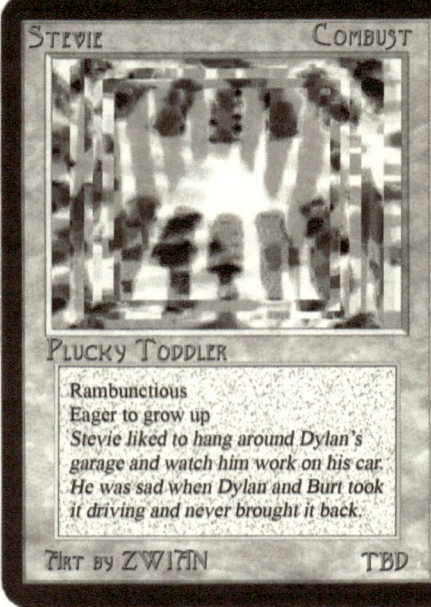

Stevie — COMBUST

PLUCKY TODDLER

Rambunctious
Eager to grow up
Stevie liked to hang around Dylan's garage and watch him work on his car. He was sad when Dylan and Burt took it driving and never brought it back.

Art by ZWIAN — TBD

COMBUST!

COLLECTIBLE CARDS

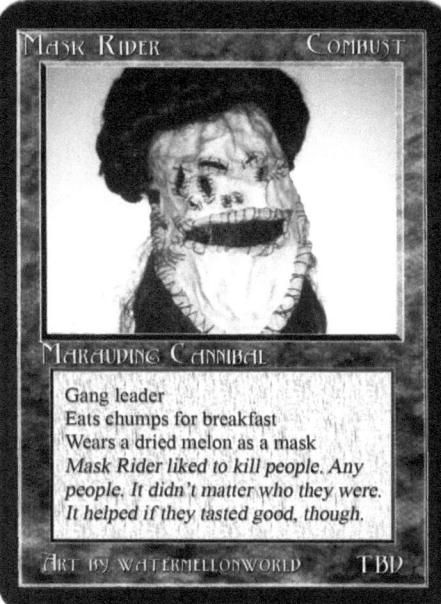

MASK RIDER · COMBUST

MARAUDING CANNIBAL

Gang leader
Eats chumps for breakfast
Wears a dried melon as a mask
Mask Rider liked to kill people. Any people. It didn't matter who they were. It helped if they tasted good, though.

ART BY WATERMELLONWORLD · TBD

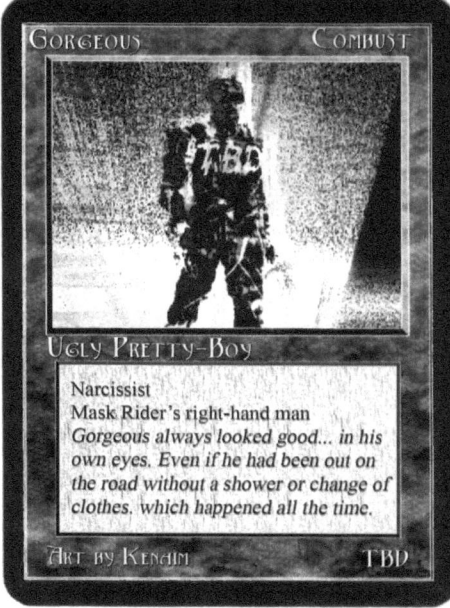

GORGEOUS · COMBUST

UGLY PRETTY-BOY

Narcissist
Mask Rider's right-hand man
Gorgeous always looked good... in his own eyes. Even if he had been out on the road without a shower or change of clothes, which happened all the time.

ART BY KENAIN · TBD

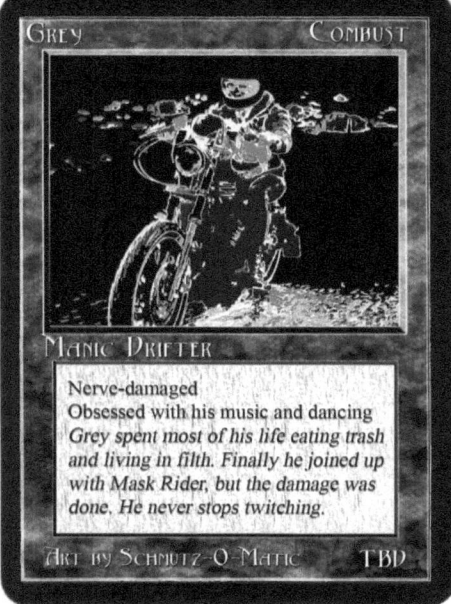

GREY · COMBUST

MANIC DRIFTER

Nerve-damaged
Obsessed with his music and dancing
Grey spent most of his life eating trash and living in filth. Finally he joined up with Mask Rider, but the damage was done. He never stops twitching.

ART BY SCHMUTZ-O-MATIC · TBD

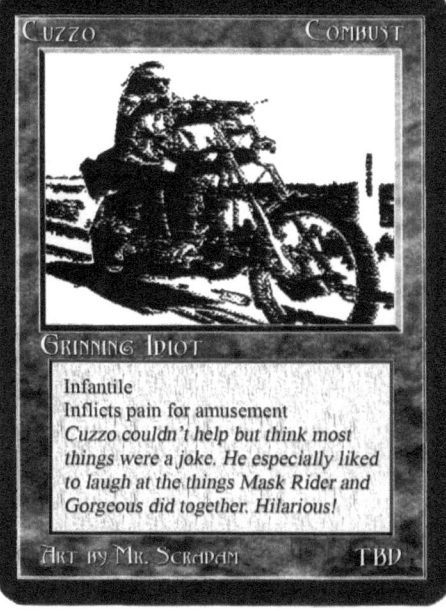

CUZZO · COMBUST

GRINNING IDIOT

Infantile
Inflicts pain for amusement
Cuzzo couldn't help but think most things were a joke. He especially liked to laugh at the things Mask Rider and Gorgeous did together. Hilarious!

ART BY MR. SCRAPAM · TBD

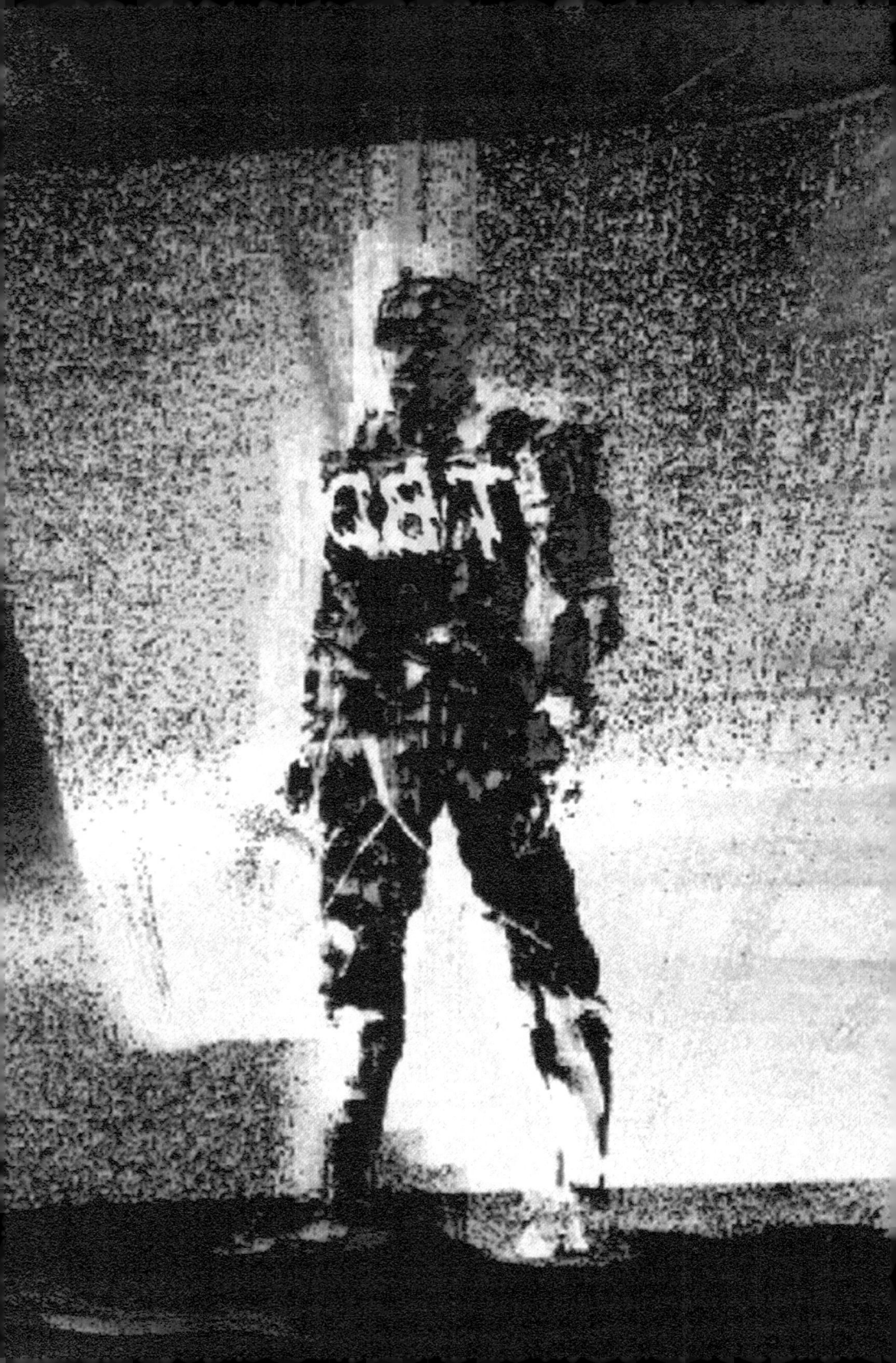

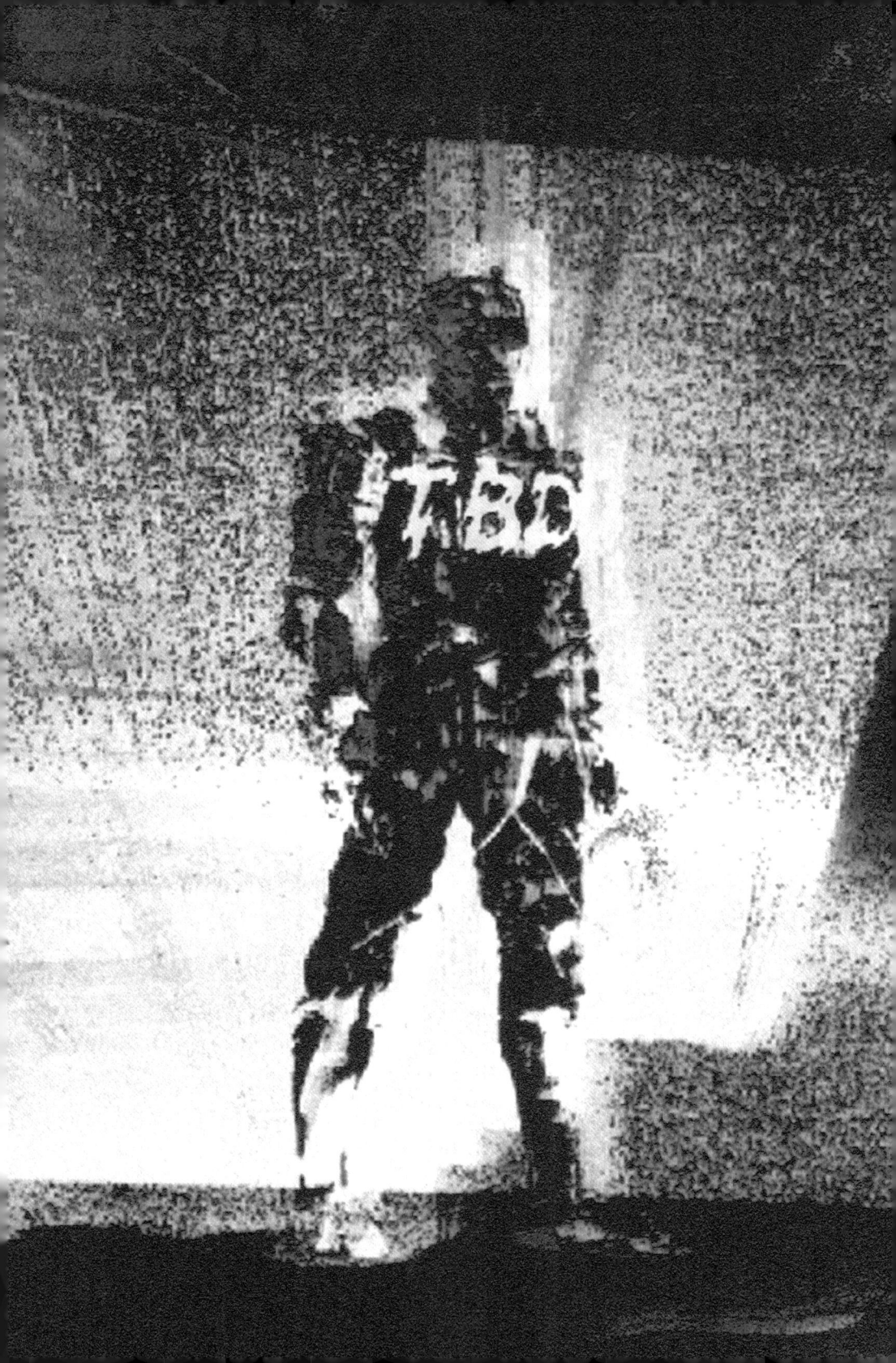

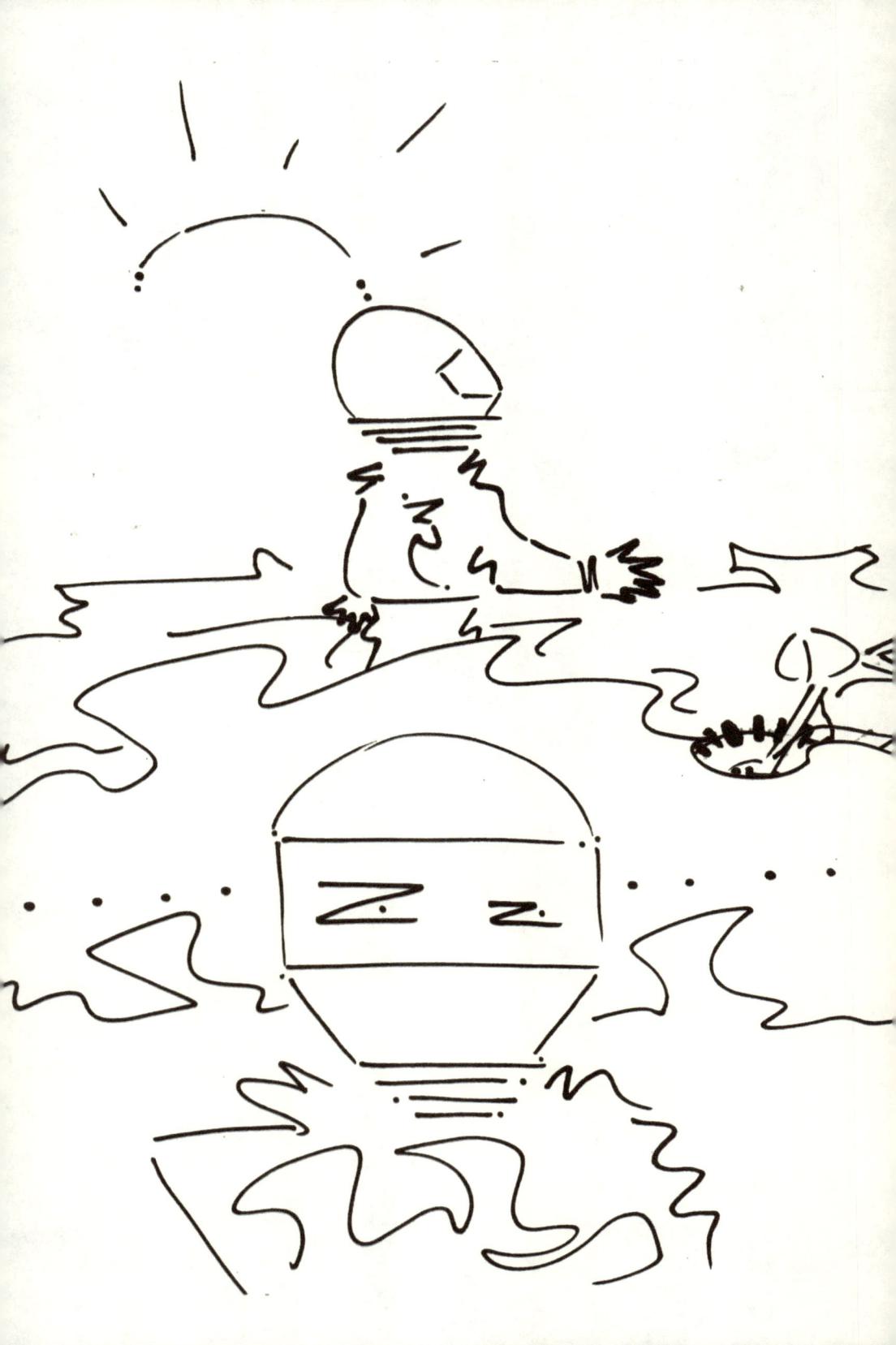

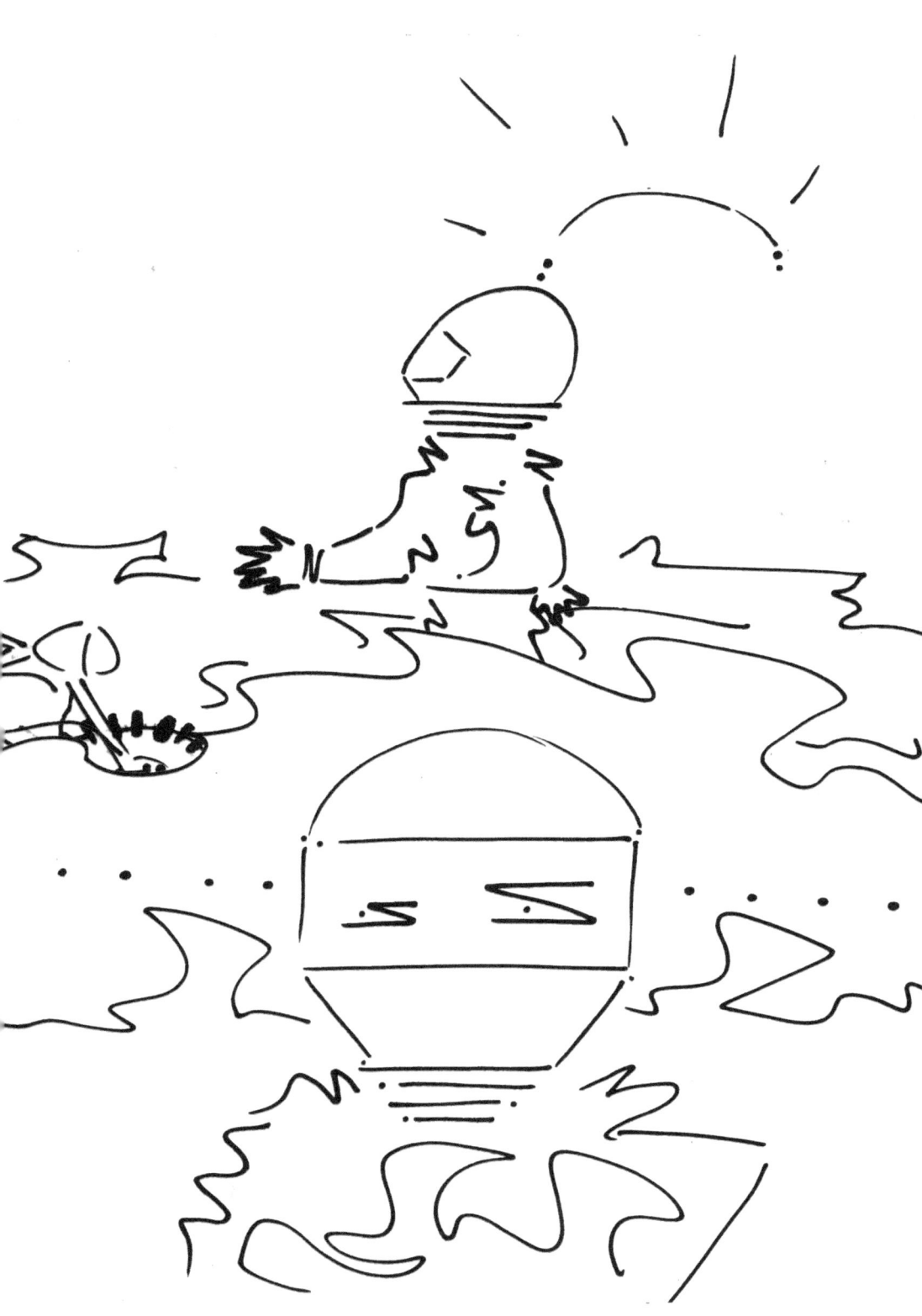

THE
BRAINCRIMES
OF
HARRIS SMITH

Harris Smith has always been a law-abiding citizen... as long as he can remember. But lately he's come to question everything he thought he knew about himself. Haunting videos, memories he can't quite place, phone calls from strangers with familiar voices - all seem to be leading him to a shocking realization.

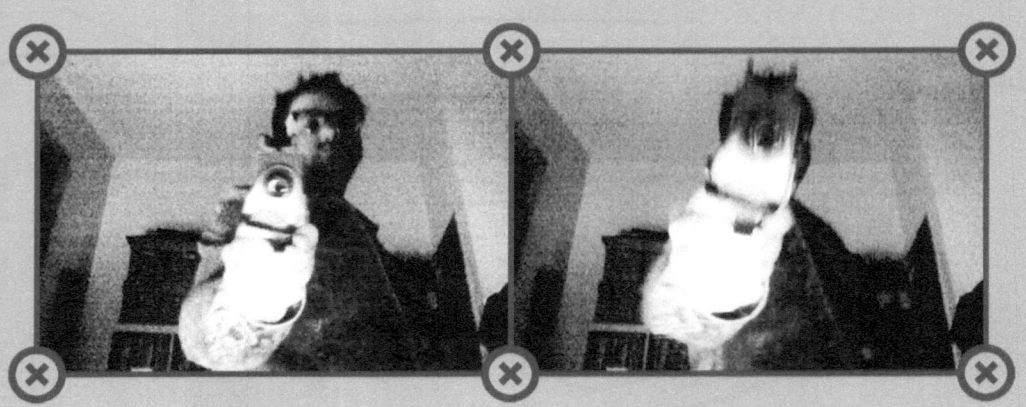

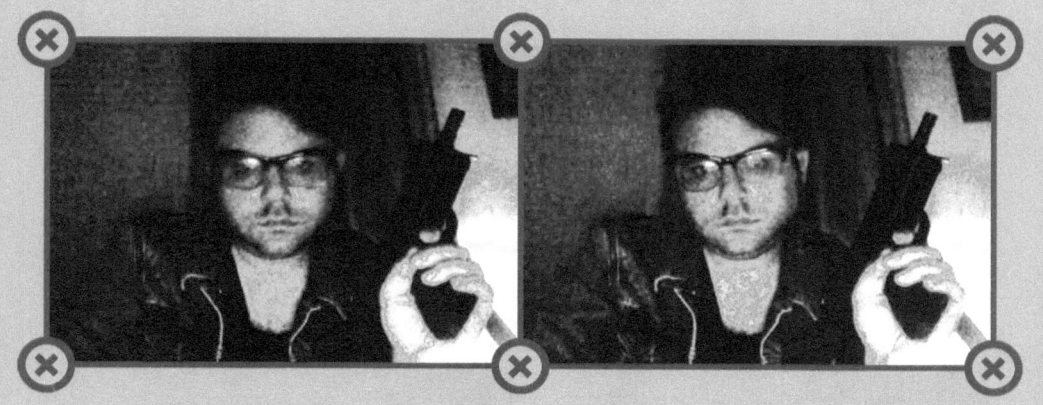

What sinister truths lay hidden in the brain of Harris Smith? What hidden menace is lurking beneath the surface, waiting to emerge? Will Harris Smith be able to outsmart the most formidable foe he has ever come across... himself? Find out in

The Braincrimes of Harris Smith

Written by Harris Smith

THE BRAINCRIMES OF HARRIS SMITH
PUBLICITY STILLS

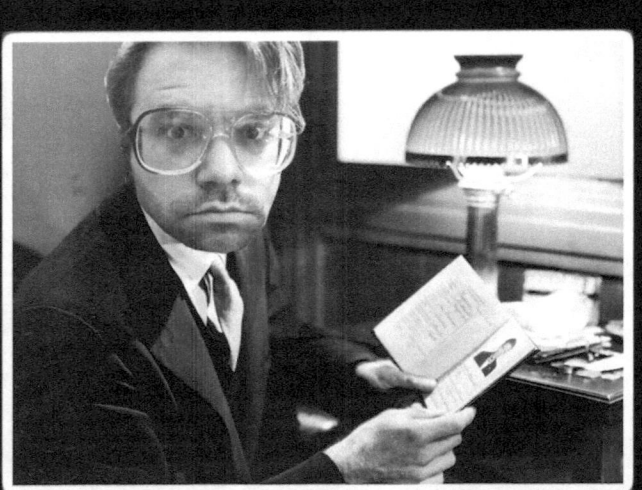

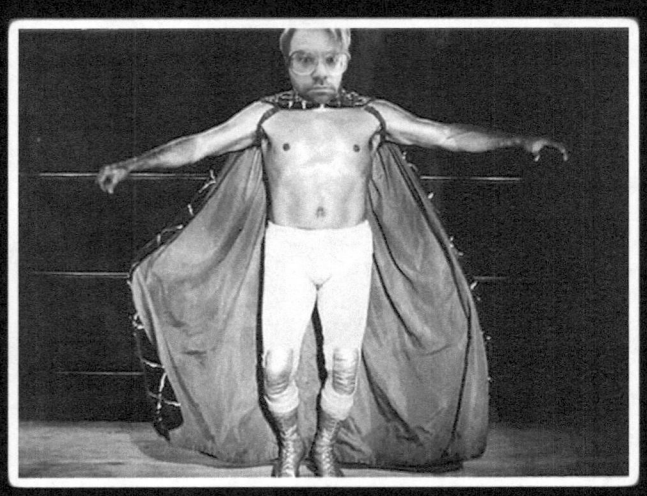

THE BRAINCRIMES OF HARRIS SMITH
PUBLICITY STILLS

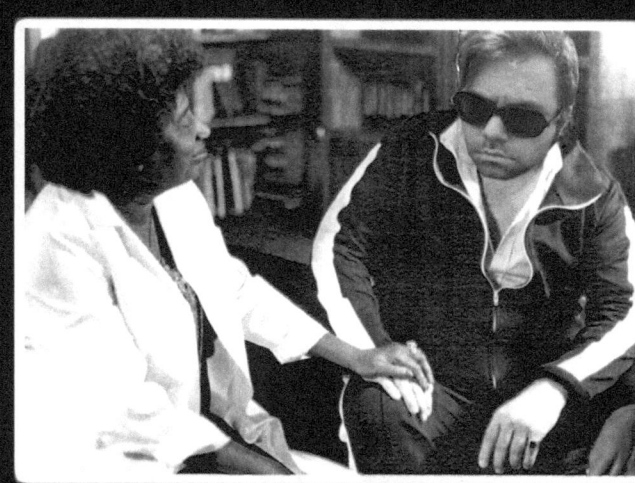

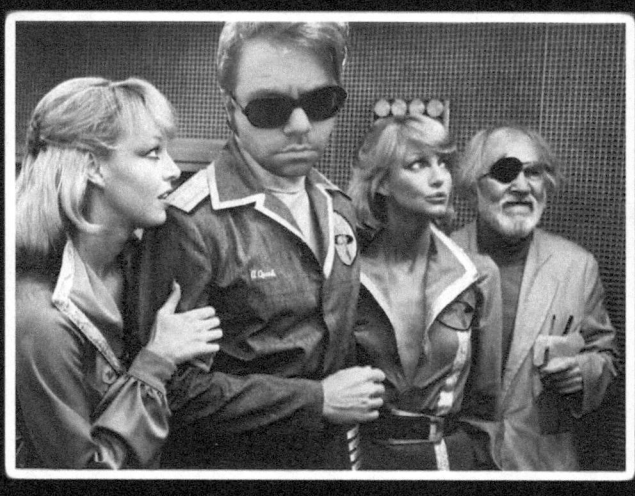

HARRIS SMITH
CUSTOMIZABLE ACTION DOLL

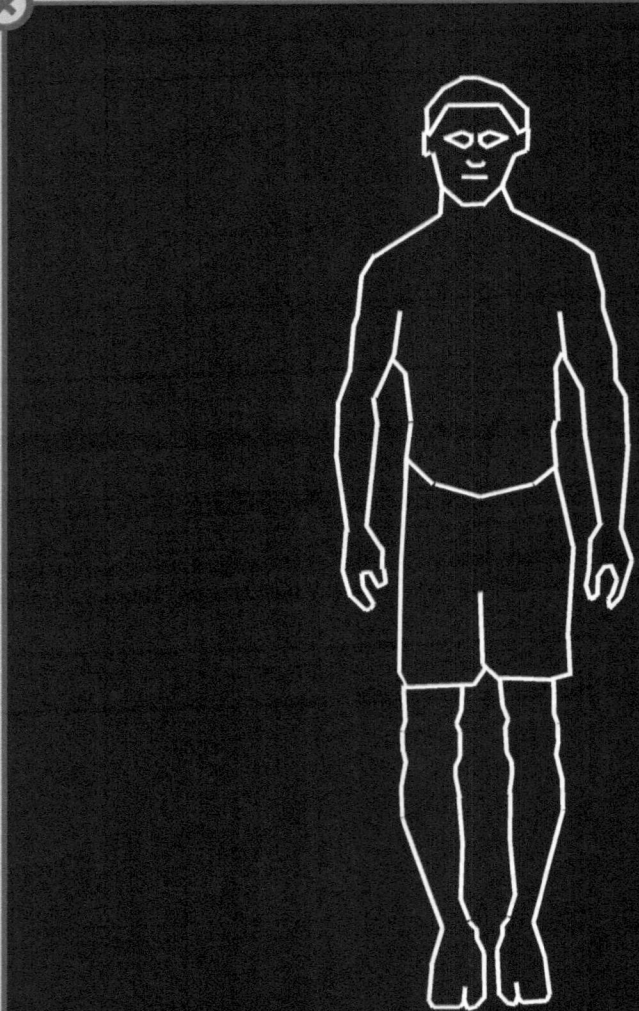

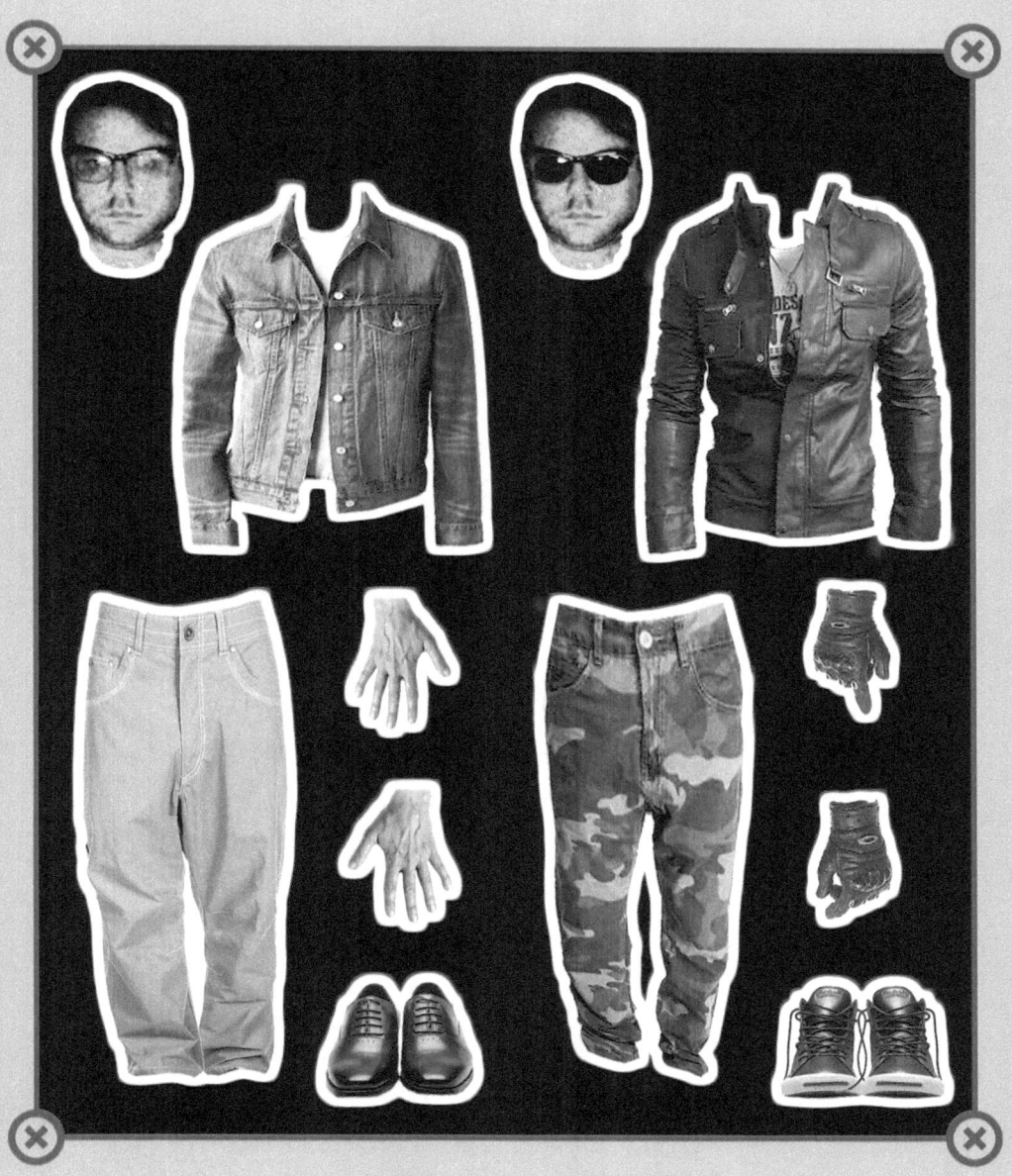

PHOTOCOPY THIS PAGE AND CUT
OUT THE SHAPES TO CUSTOMIZE
YOUR HARRIS SMITH ACTION DOLL

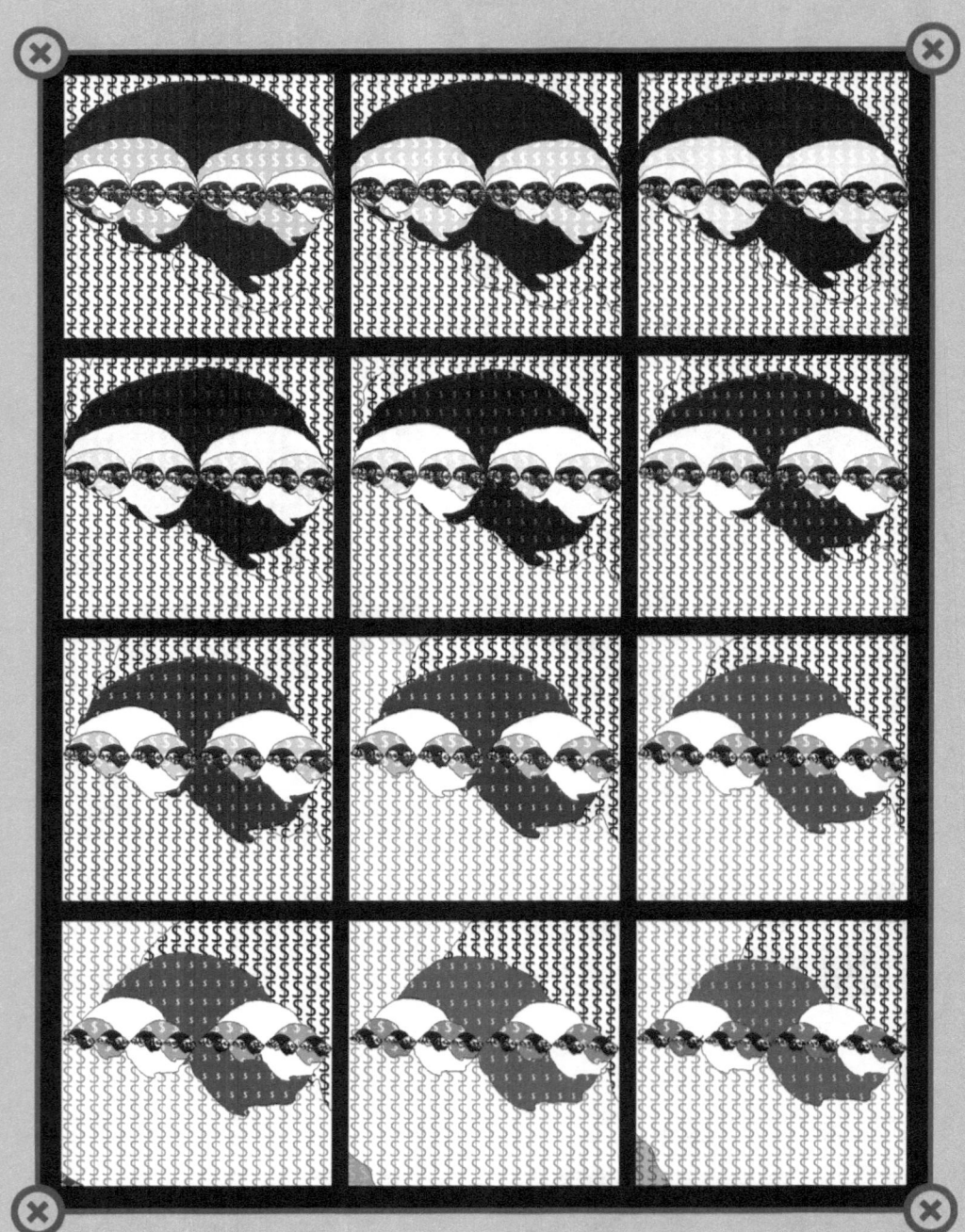

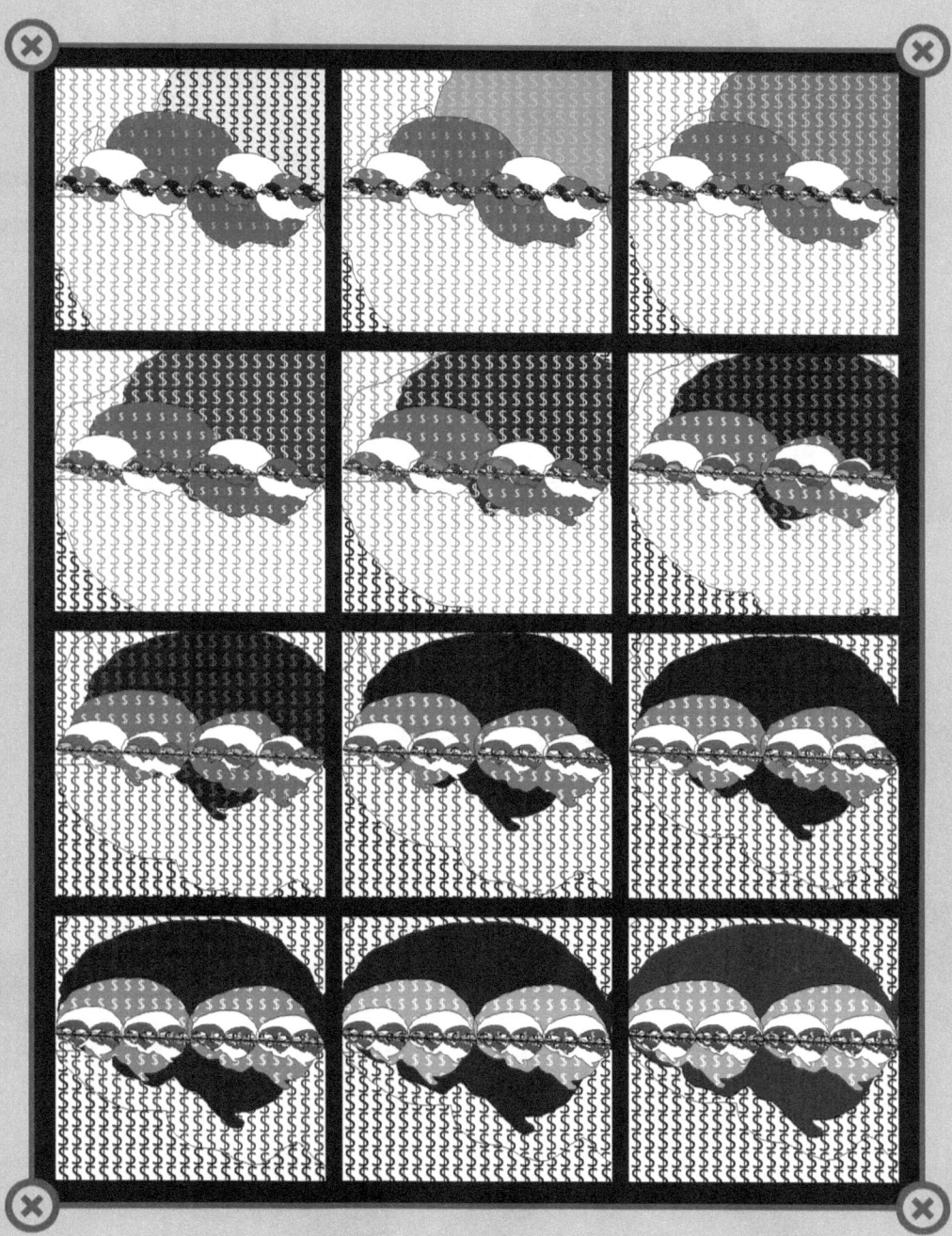

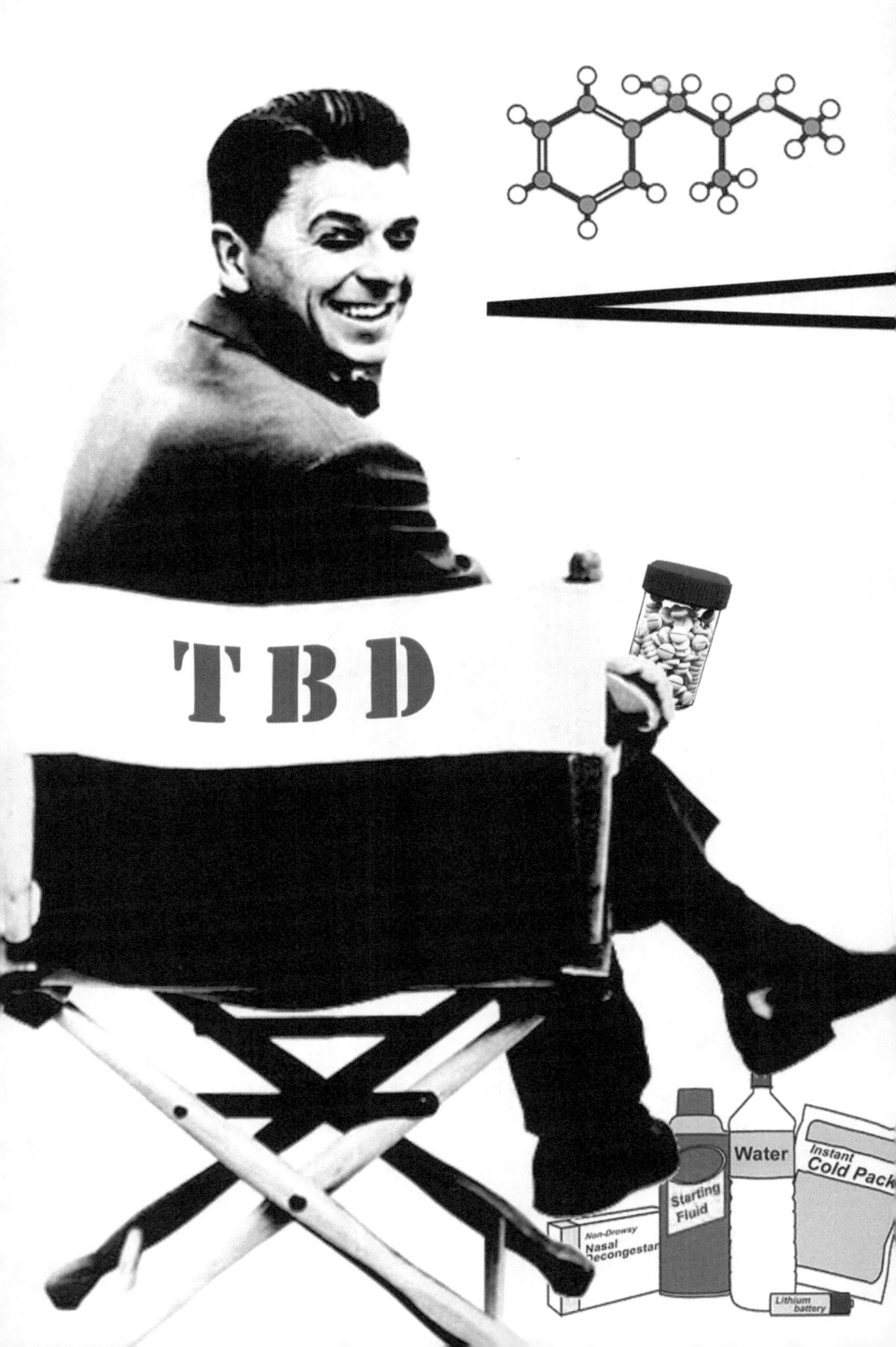

YAWN! We made it thru all of those fabulous stories. Thank you for sticking with us! Something tells me that we will all need some serious supplements to keep us alert during the movie. I... uh... no... the people at GE wont appreciate glib comments like that. Let us not forget who we are. Drug abuse is a repudiation of everything America is. Please enjoy some work by some fine young artists... members of TBD.

By Zach W
zwian.tumblr.com

COLORING GIF

Instructions: Draw, Color, or Alter the Frames on this page by any preffered method then scan or photograph the page and sequence the frames as a gif.

If you can't or don't know how to make a gif send me a scan of your page and I'll make it for you, zwiagd@gmail.com Have fun!

SATANIC SUDOKU

			6		6			6
	6	6					6	6
				6				6
6			6		6			
					6		6	6
6	6					6	6	
		6		6				

Hint: Just use the number 6!

FIND WORDS

```
B I Z L C H T Z V X P
R L Q Z O A V Y V U T
A D O S N R S W B F D
I Y N X L R M L B K V
N C E B V I I A E P O
C O M B U S T E N E Z
R R W D H T H D Q M P
I M M I J U B E F O N O
M Z N S E D V D U O W
E G C A A Y Q S T I E
S R Y S O N E B N Z F
```

Hint: Find words!

TBD:THE MAZE

Start

End

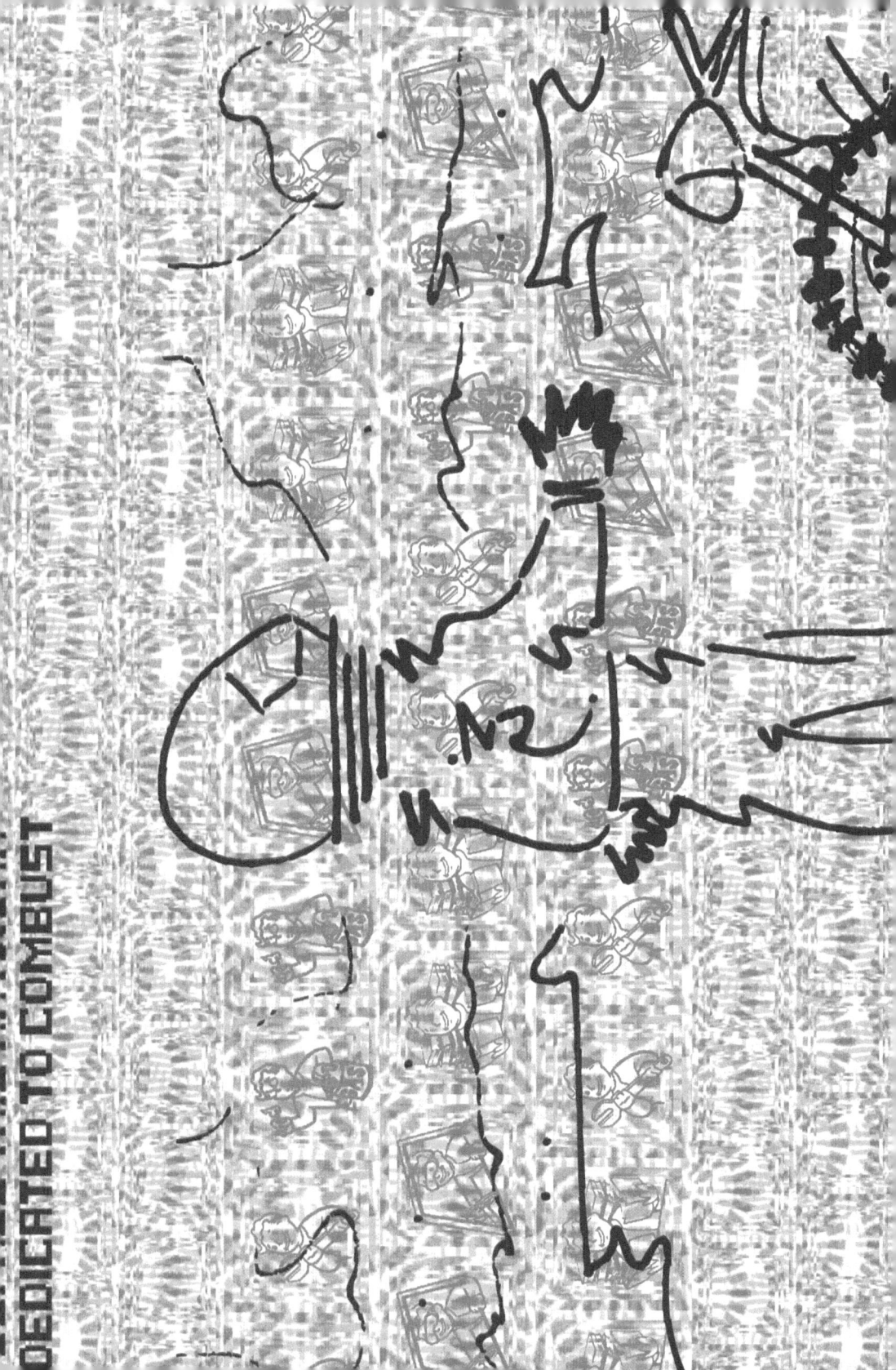

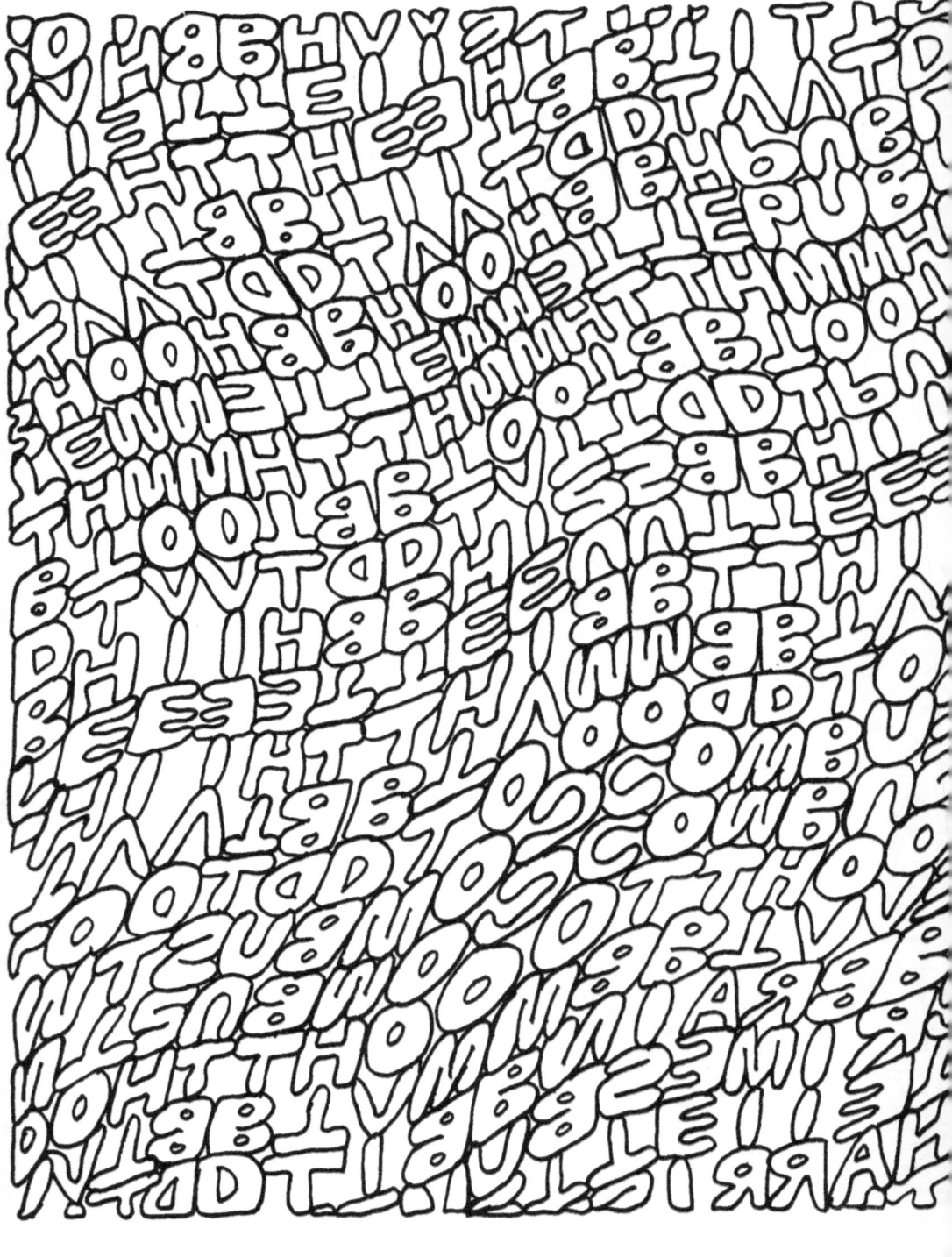

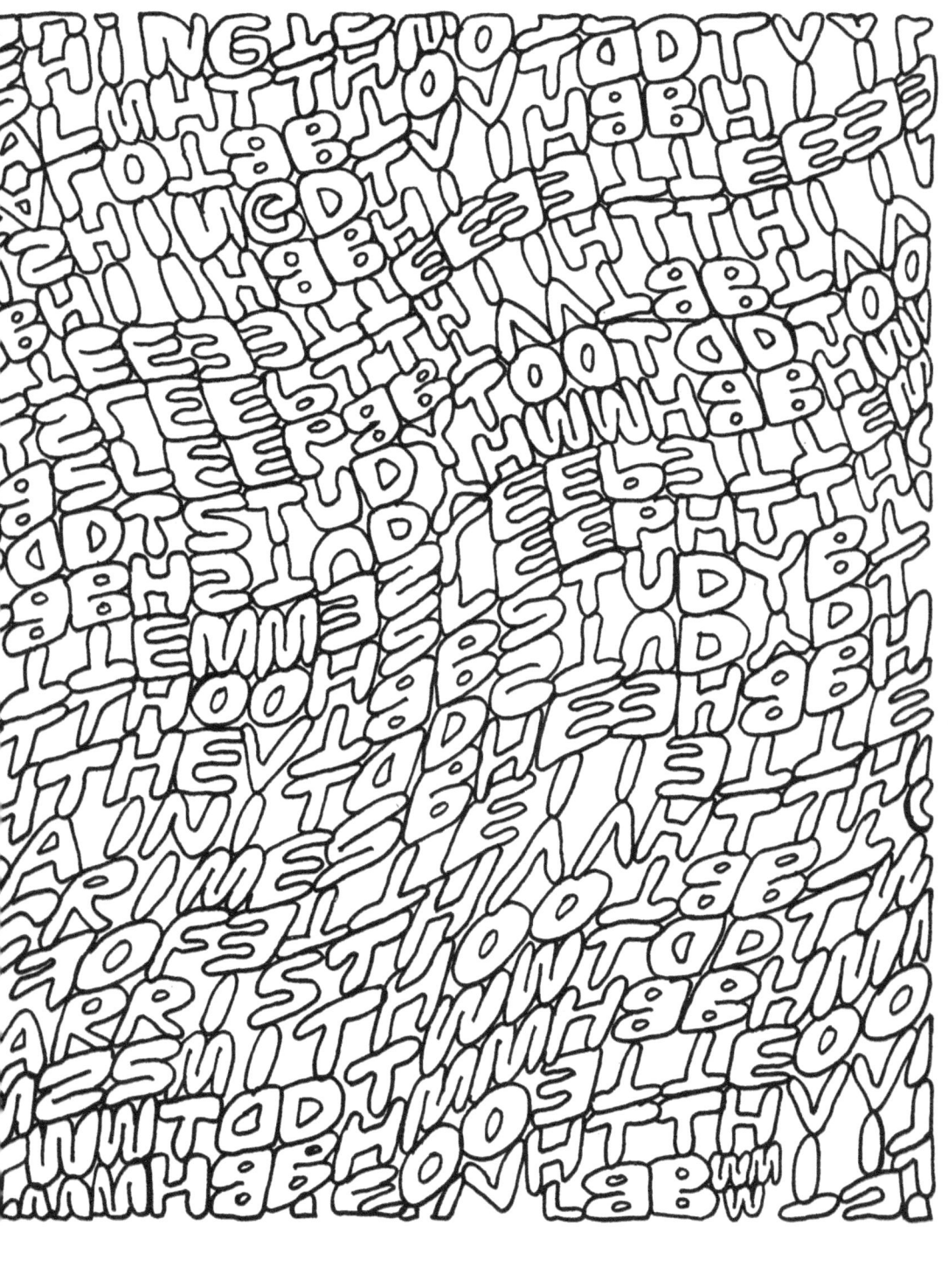

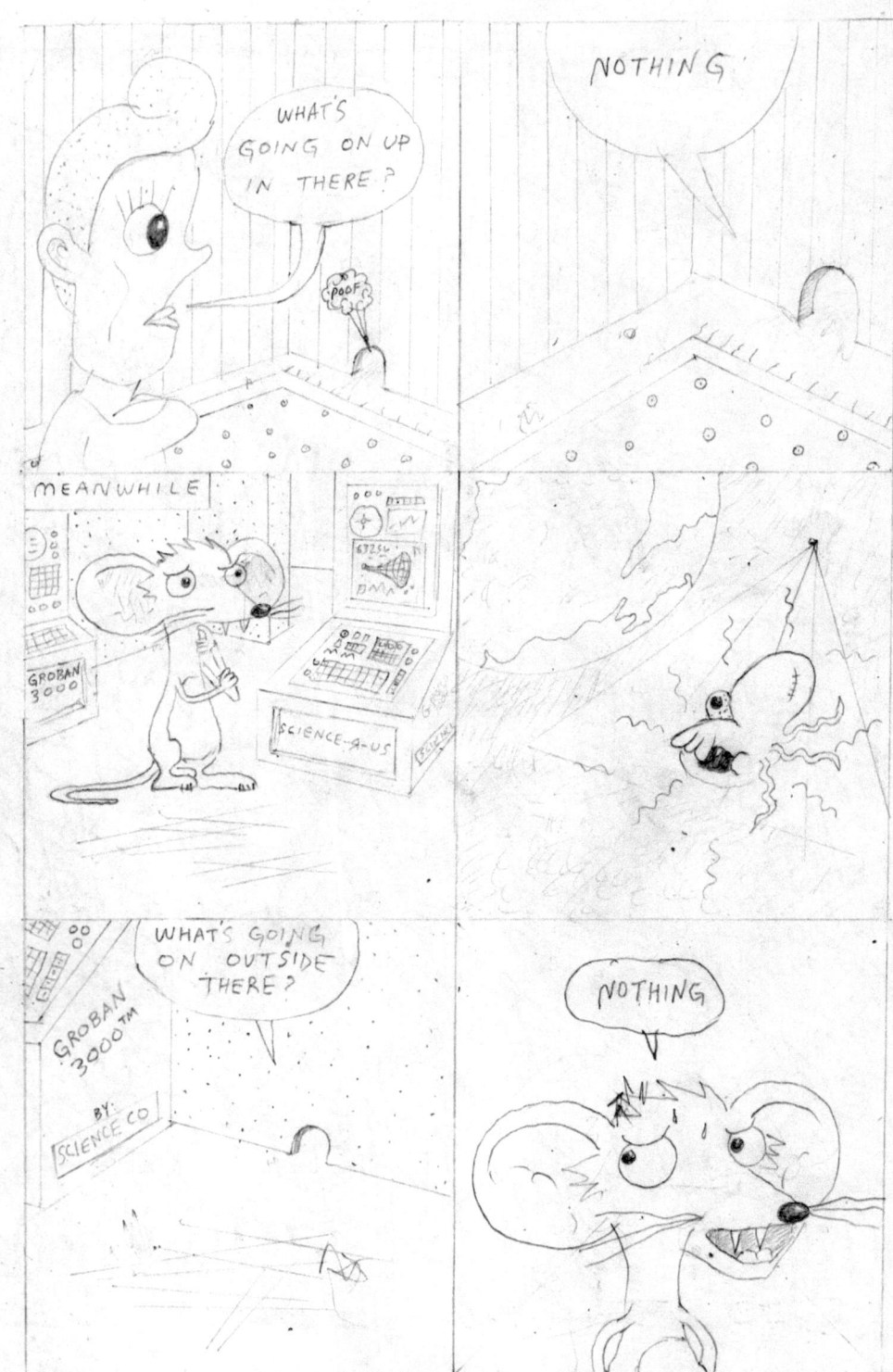

KNOWLEDGEKNIGHT FOUND THE MOST
EVIL CASTLE TO STORM ON CRAIGSLIST

THE FIRST THRESHOLD HAD TO BE TOLD
A JOKE FUNNY ENOUGH TO OPEN DOORWAY

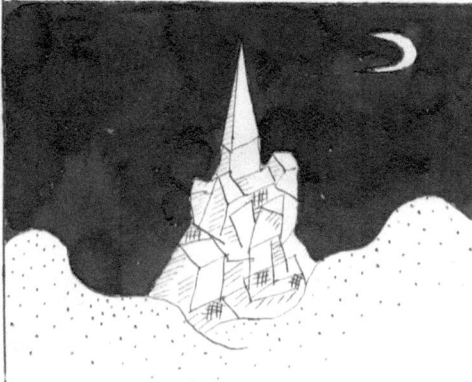

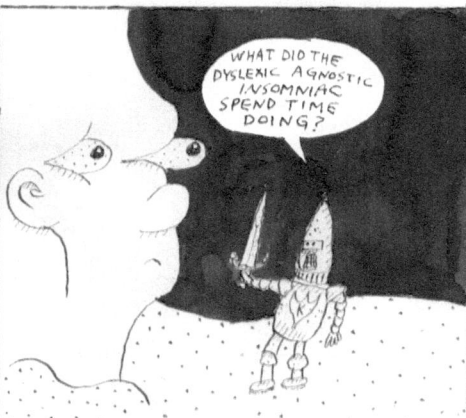

THE SECOND...INSIDE THE EVIL CASTLE
WAS EASY AS IT WAS LEFT OPEN

OR SO IT SEEMED.. OUR HERO FOUND
HERSELF CONSUMED WITH TERRORS

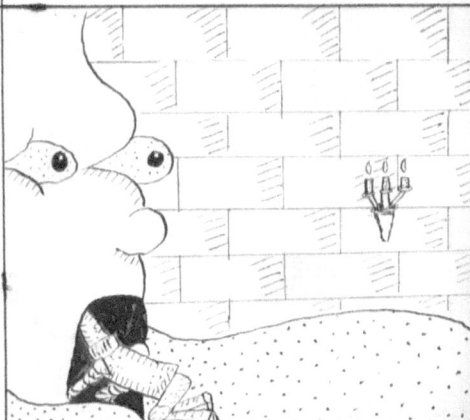

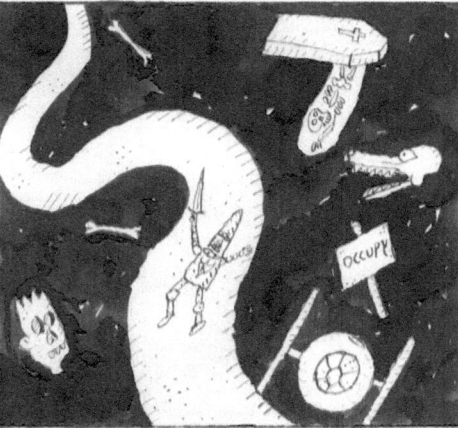

NOT UNLIKE AN ANT TRAPPED INSIDE
JOAN RIVERS INDUSTRIAL STRENGTH VIBRATOR

THE FINAL BATTLE WAS WITH THE
GEORDI LA FORGE DRAGON BOSS

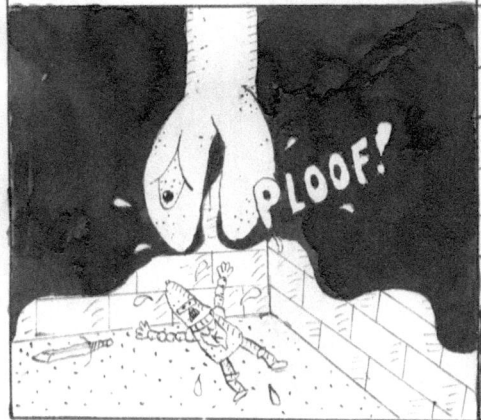

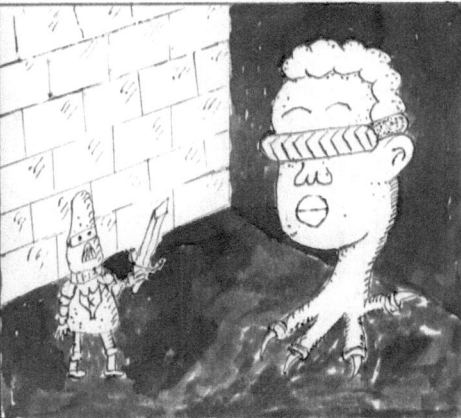

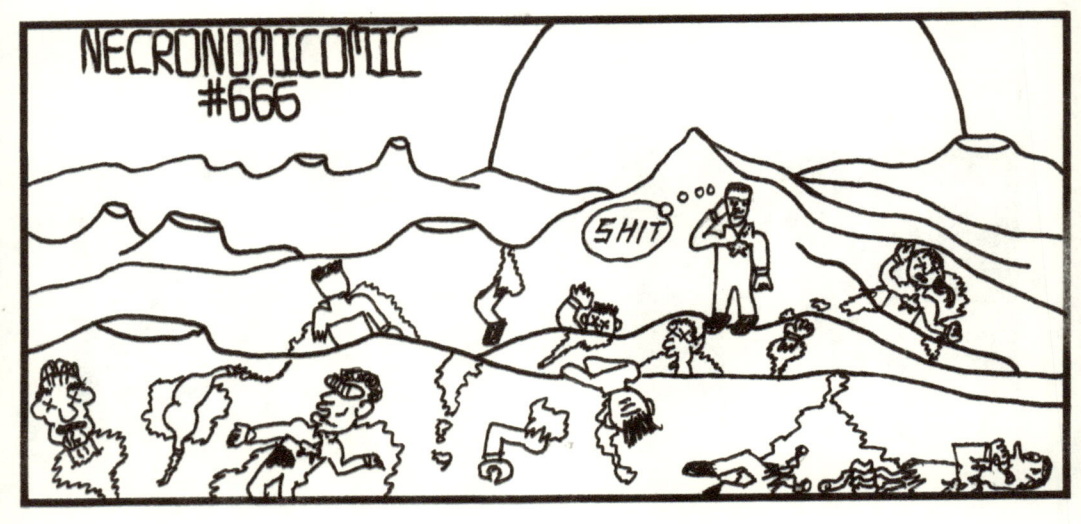

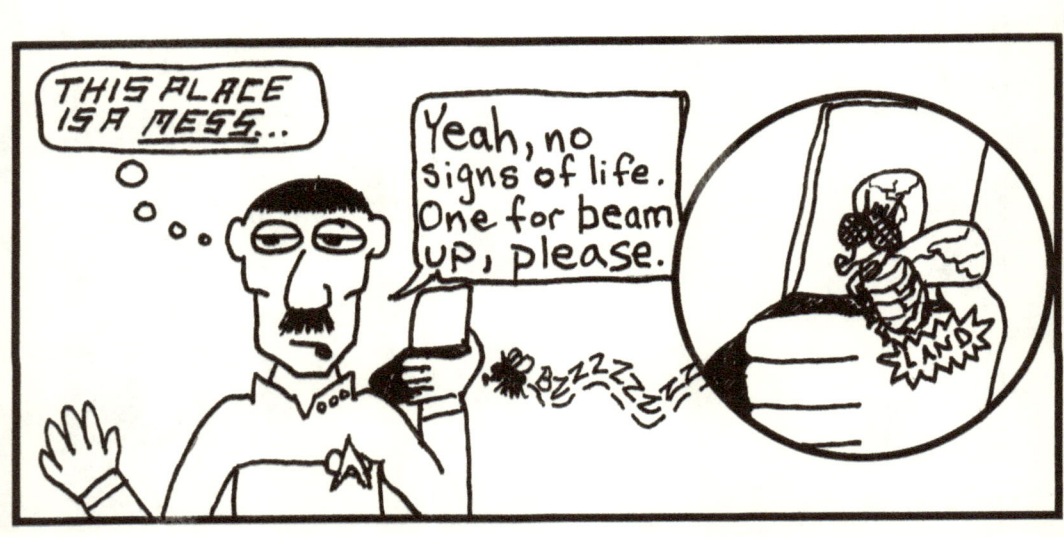

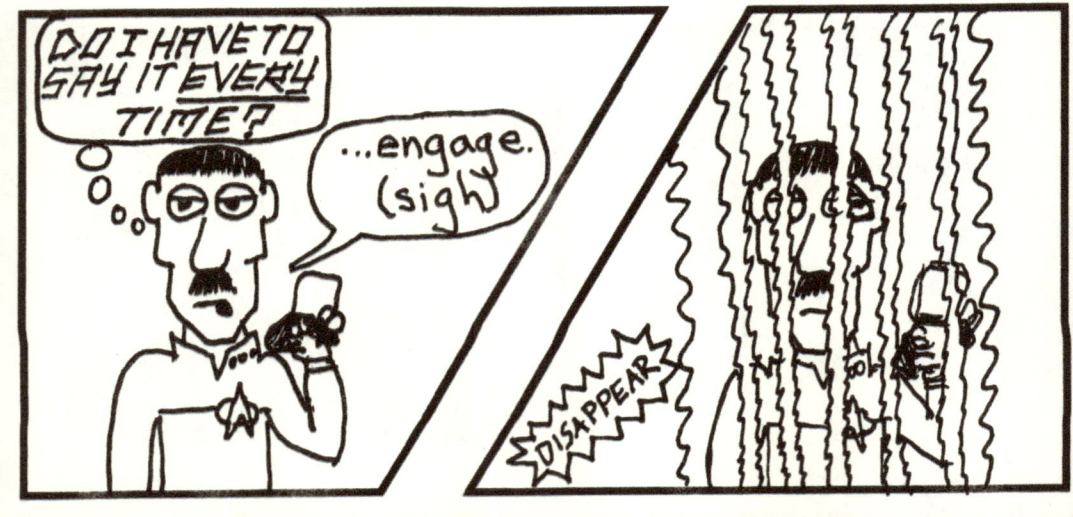

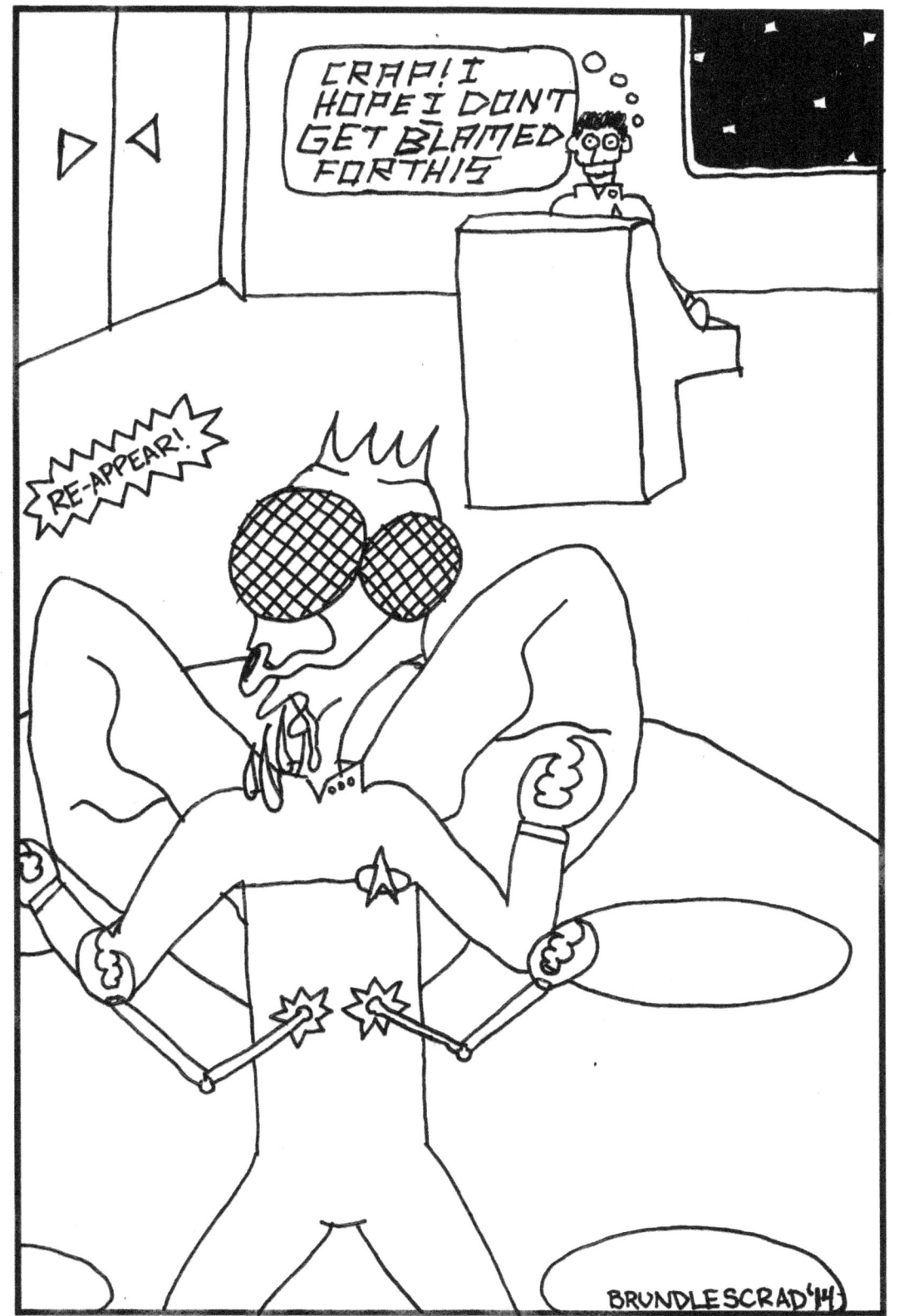

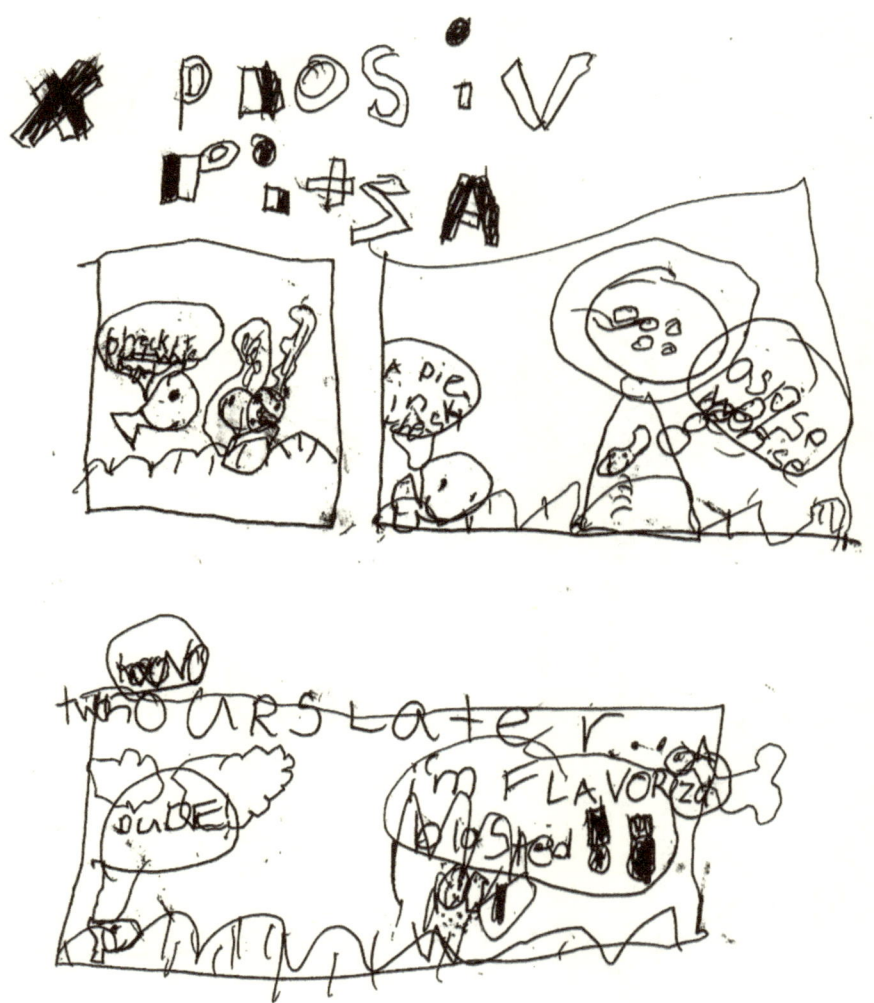

necronomicomic #8

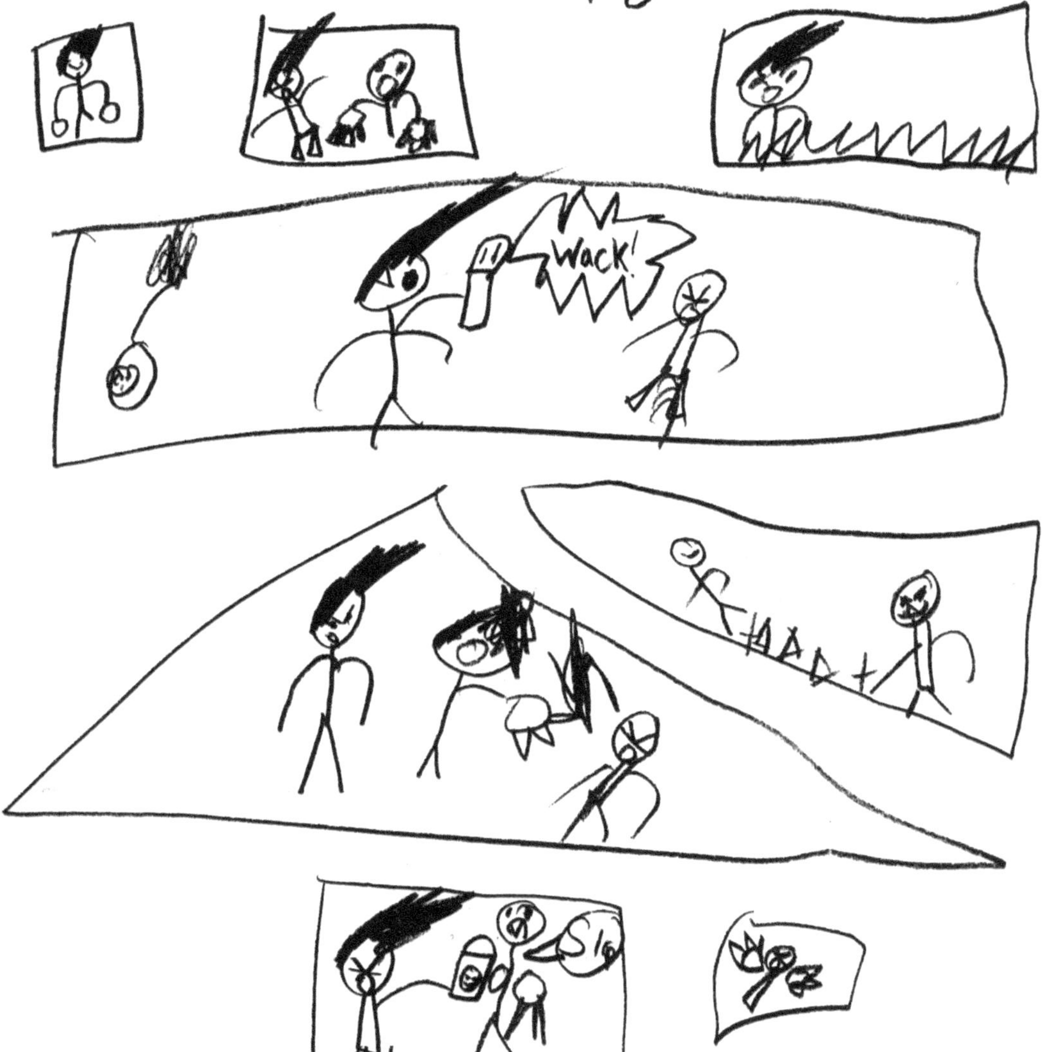

WACK!

the end

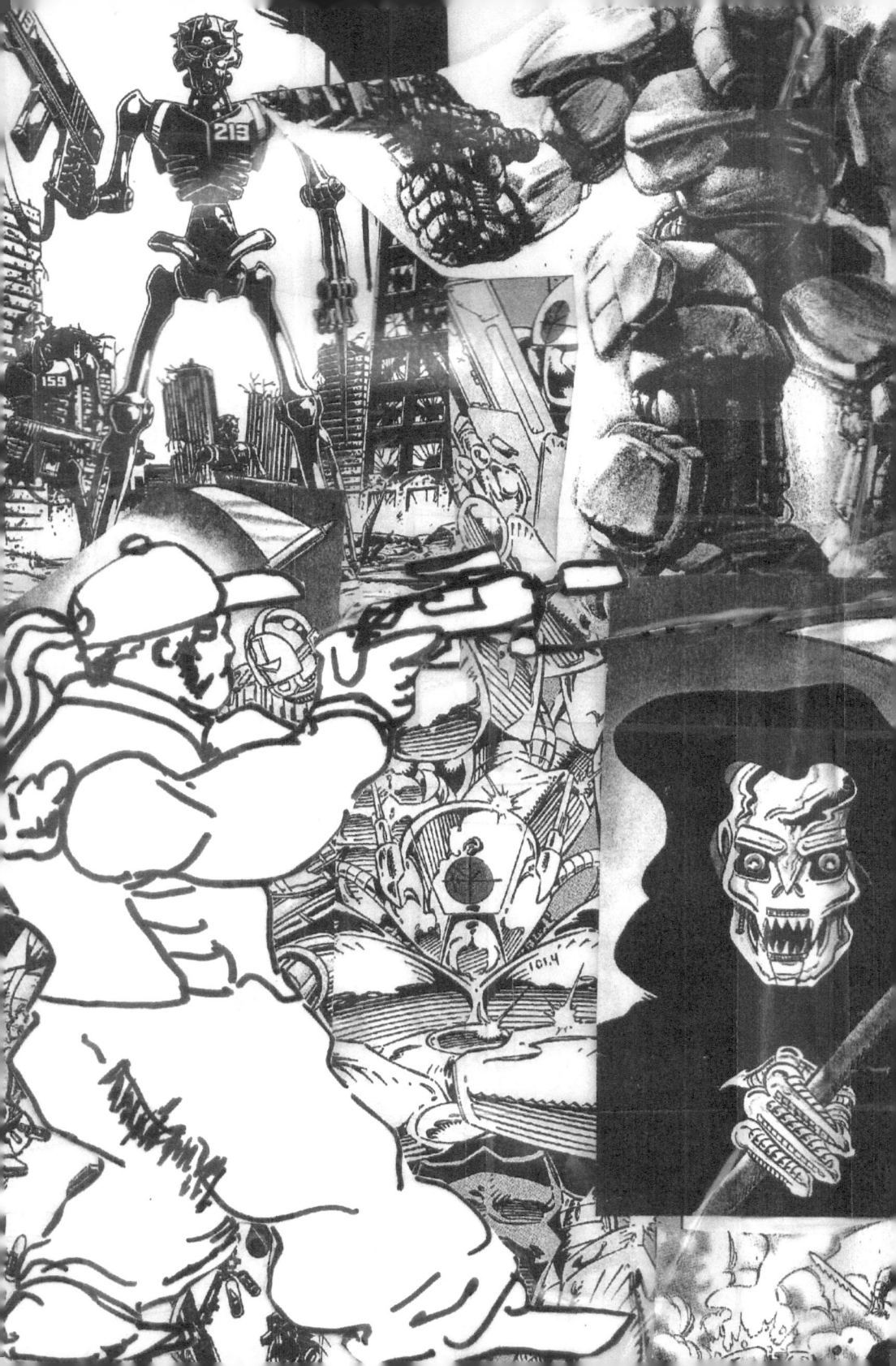

YES, WELL, YOU CAN JUST CALL ME "THE JELLY BEAN MAN"

Reagan pulls a small pillbox from his pocket. He crushes the pill into a glass of water sitting on an endtable next to him. He splashes the glass of water into his own face then SIGHS WITH RELIEF...

GIANT TALKING CELERY: "MAY I ASK?"

RONALD REAGAN: "IT'S AN ORGANIC SUPPLEMENT. JUST A LITTLE SOMETHING FOR MY SKIN"

TBD: The Movie

COMING SOON TO SOME SCREEN NEAR YOU

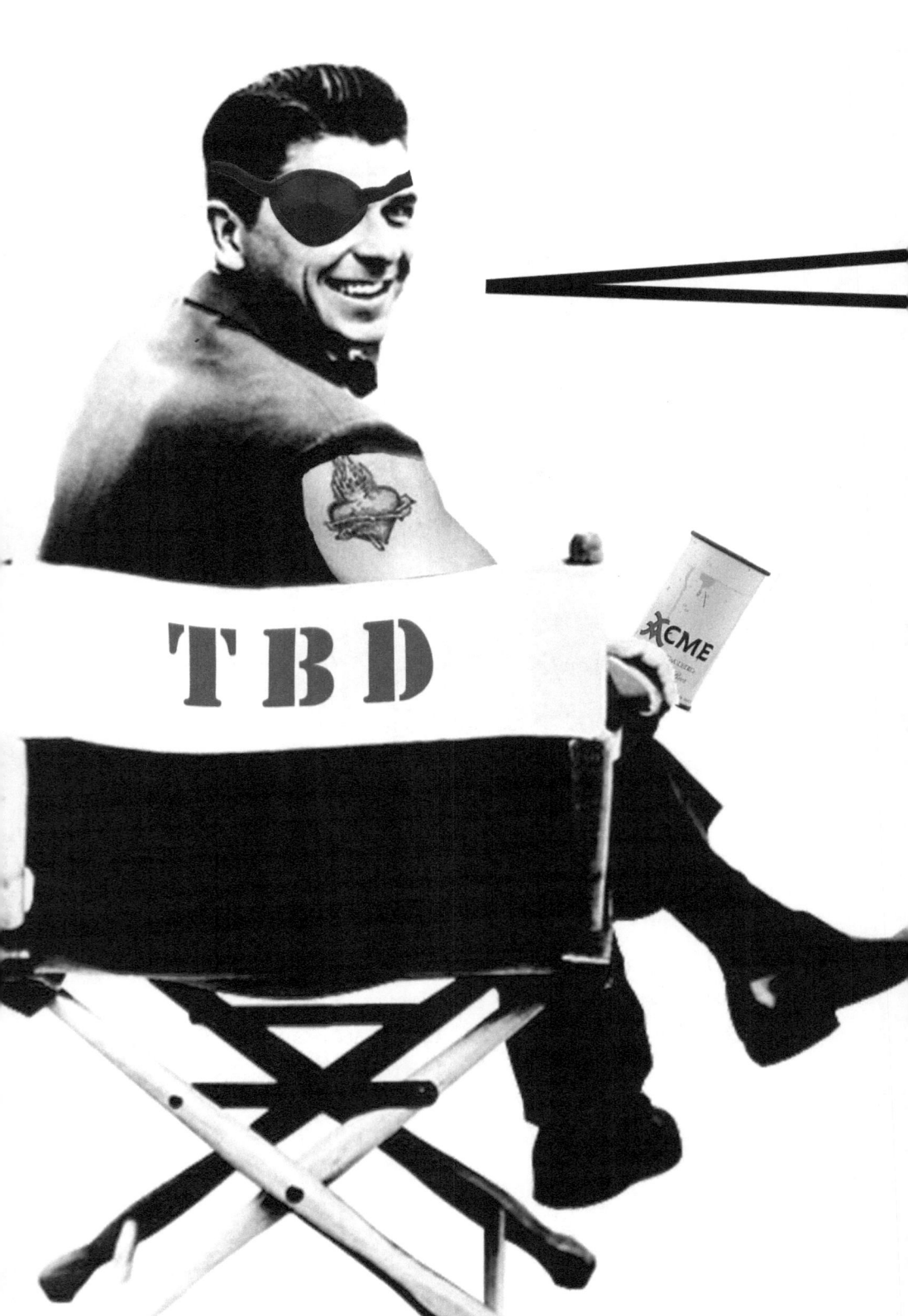

Jeepers! The folks at TBD are working hard to show you fantastic art! Its true hard work never killed anybody but I figure why take the chance? Id rather sit back and watch the show unfold. Its about time someone made a good movie. Folks in Hollywood dont make them like they used to. But movies take money to make! Please consider soliciting one of the services on the next pages to show your support.

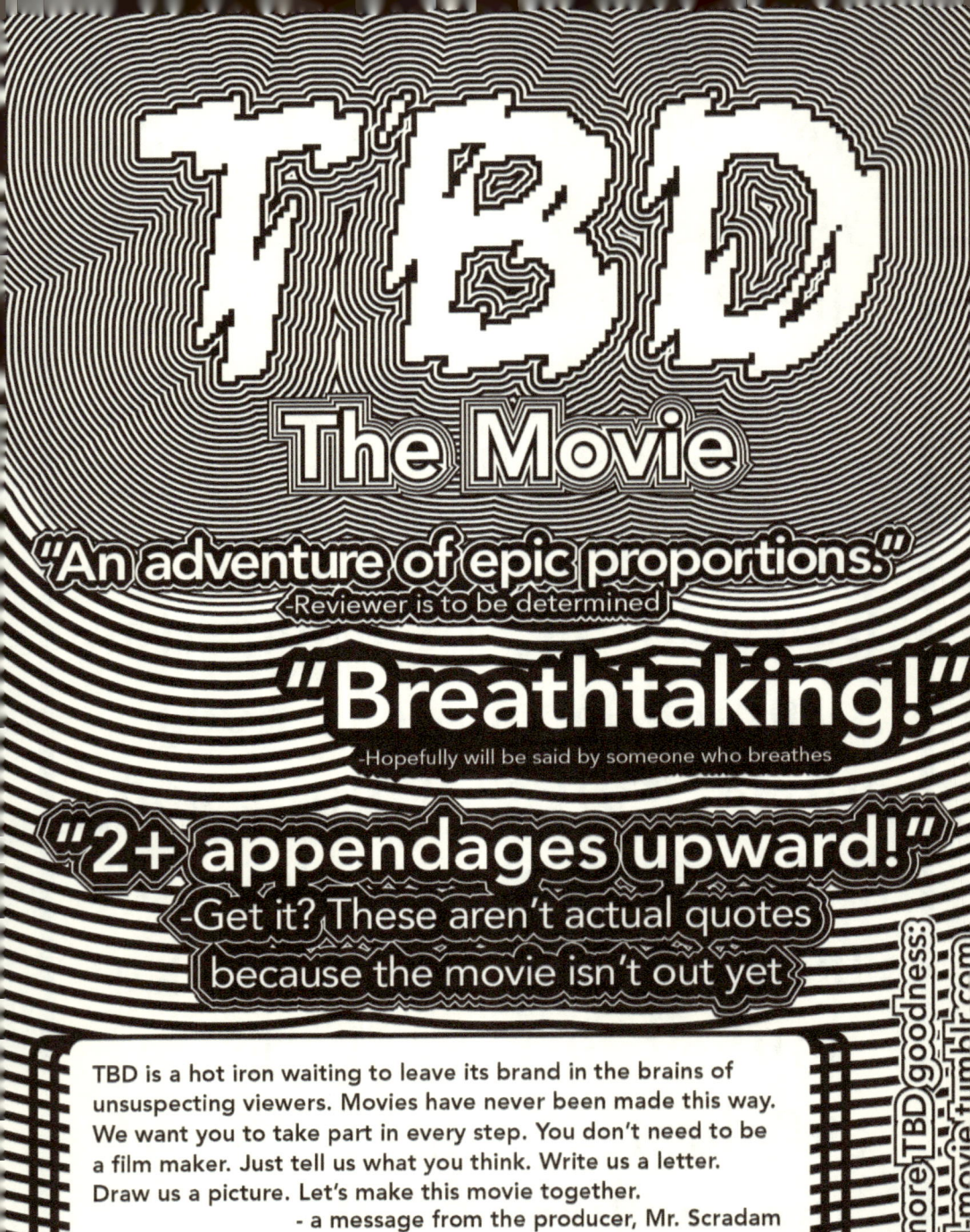

TBD

The Movie

"An adventure of epic proportions."
-Reviewer is to be determined

"Breathtaking!"
-Hopefully will be said by someone who breathes

"2+ appendages upward!"
-Get it? These aren't actual quotes
because the movie isn't out yet

TBD is a hot iron waiting to leave its brand in the brains of unsuspecting viewers. Movies have never been made this way. We want you to take part in every step. You don't need to be a film maker. Just tell us what you think. Write us a letter. Draw us a picture. Let's make this movie together.
- a message from the producer, Mr. Scradam

What he said.
- a message from the guy who made this page, Zach W.

for more TBD goodness:
thbmovie.tumblr.com

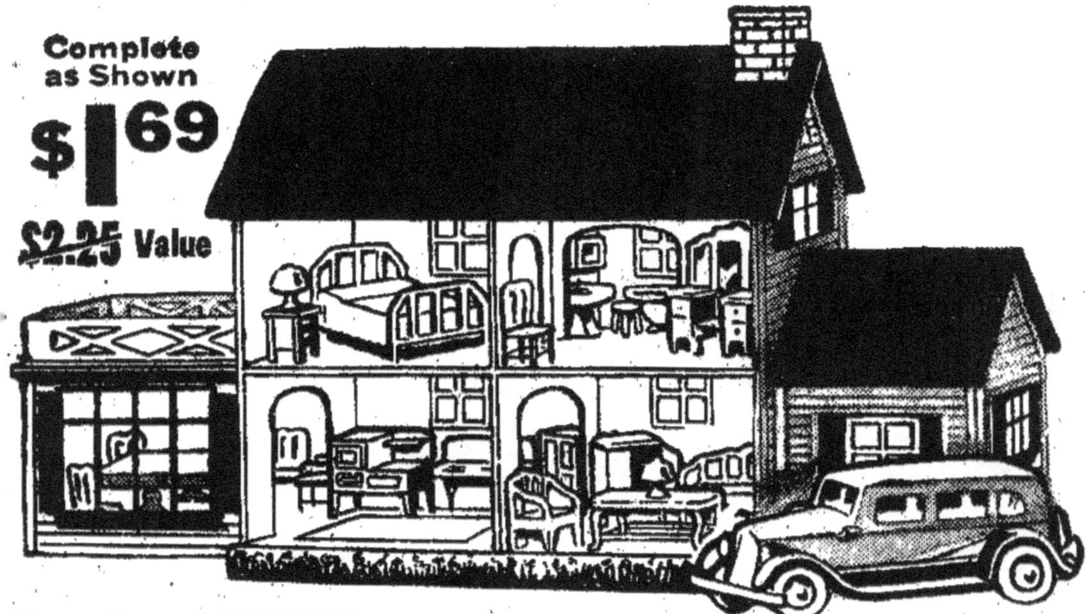

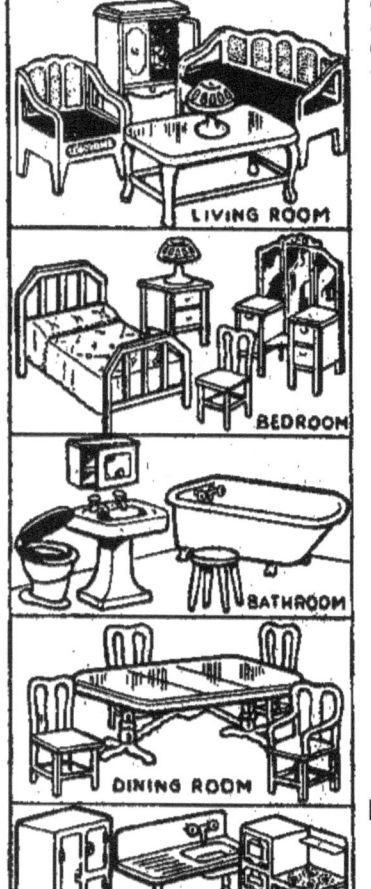
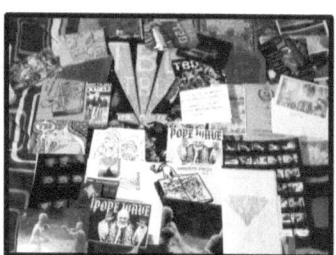
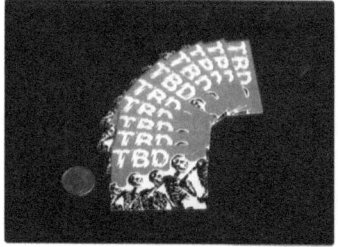

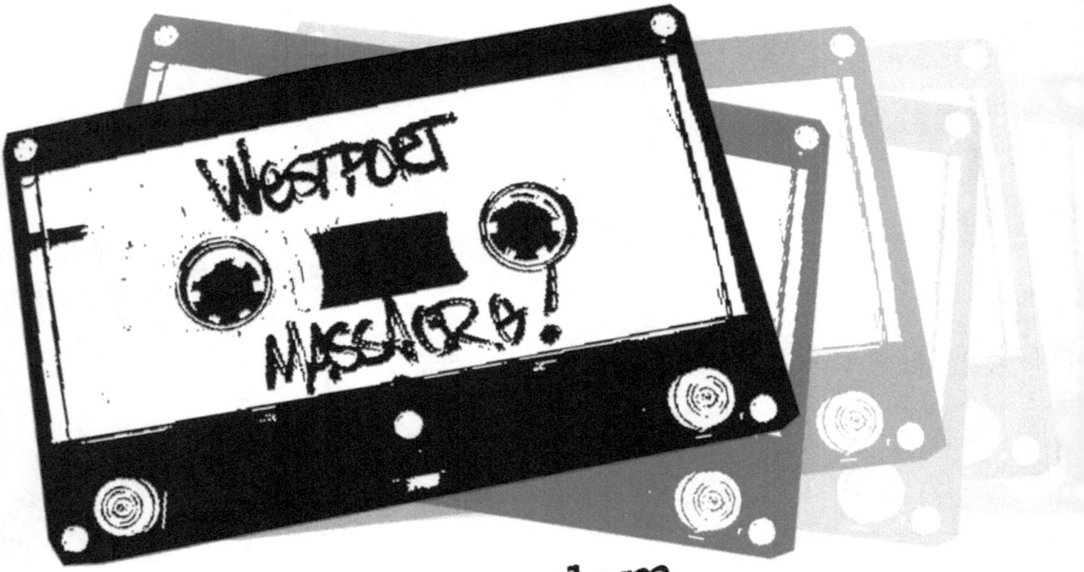

ZWIAN vs Mr. Scradam
The Westport Massacre

A collab album and limited edition tape that has people saying

"sick beats <3"
- dzumeister.tumblr.com

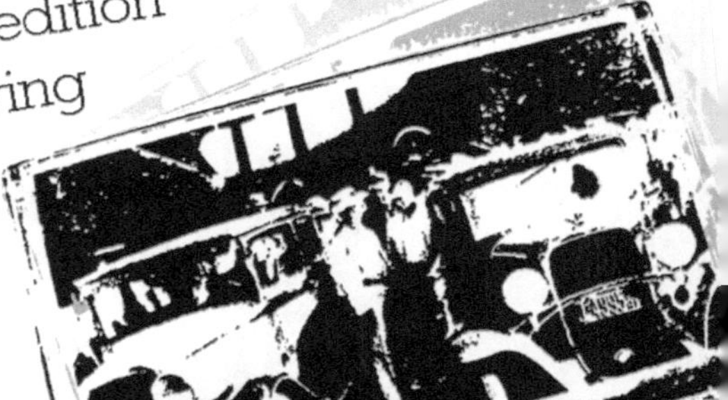

"If you're ready for some beats that you can fight to (Please, don't hurt each other. Let's bring back breakdancing instead) then this is the tape for you to put in your ghetto blaster."
- raisedbygypsies.com

Available now at
tbdthemixtape.bandcamp.com

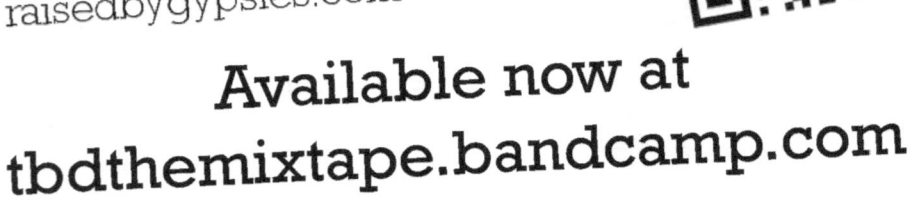

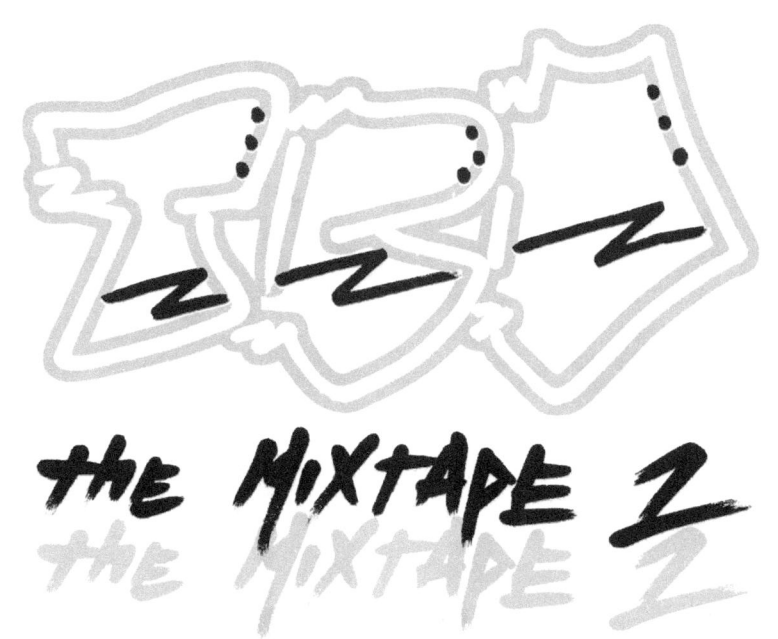

the MiXTAPE 2

tracks by
tho tway /// KUWAIT /// FAILSAFE!
ünderNøøm+ /// Therazoredge
C. Vadi /// Fish Titan /// ENDOR
Zach Is Sleeping /// The TV People
terlu

art by
Mr. Scradam /// ZWIAN /// Therazoredge
Kenaim /// Max Capacity
Schmutz-O-Matic

Also available now at
tbdthemixtape.bandcamp.com

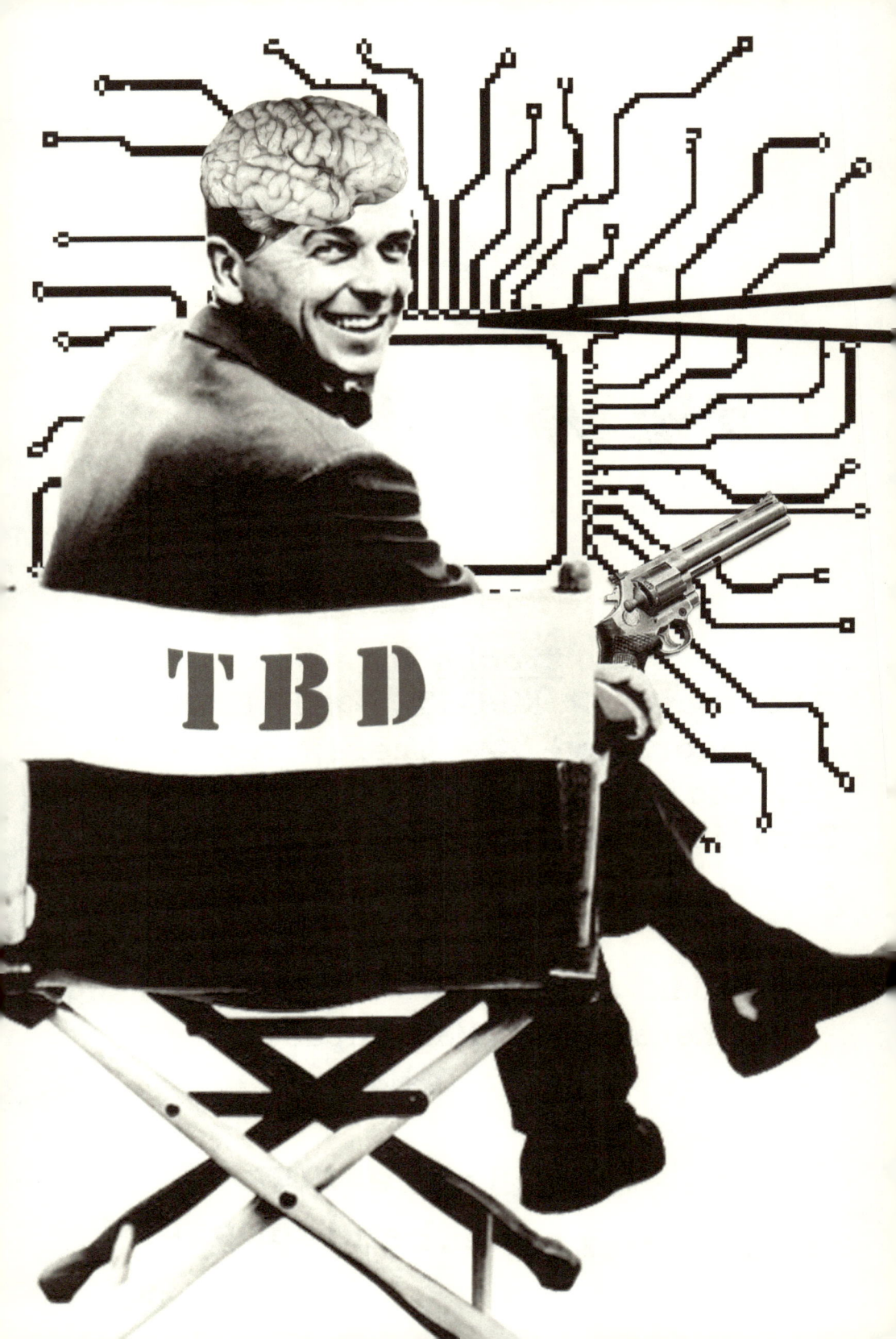

Have you ever had an urge to do something strange? If you read this zine Im sure you have! Thanks for following your strange urge to delve into the world of TBD. The zine is not the end of the fun. Check out

TBD The Mixtape...
TBD The Mixtape 2...
TBD House of swag...
And TBD The Movie.

Coming soon to a computer screen near you!

Dont forget to support the artists involved. Cheers!

TBD THE MOVIE

WOULD LIKE TO THANK THE FOLLOWING ARTISTS
FOR MAKING THIS ZINE POSSIBLE

COVER AND TV COLLAGE

ZWIAN

RONALD REAGAN SCRIPT QUOTABLES

WATERMELLONWORLD

PUBLISHING DEAL POSTER

TOM GARRETT

PUBLISHING DEAL SYNOPSIS AND CAST LIST

WORDS BY TOM GARRETT

PUBLISHING DEAL SCENE & STORYBOARD

MIKE KRONBERGER

COMBUST SYNOPSIS

MR. SCRADAM AND SCHMUTZ-O-MATIC
ILLUSTRATION BY WATERMELLONWORLD

COMBUST GORGEOUS CONCEPT ART

KENAIM

COMBUST HELEN CONCEPT ART

SCHMUTZ-O-MATIC

HARRIS SMITH SELF-PORTRAITS

HARRIS SMITH

BRAINCRIMES GIF SPREAD

GIF BY ENCHANTED CONSOLE

ZWIANS ACTIVITY PAGES

ZWIAN

DEFACE THIS ARTWORK

REMIX BY ZWIAN
ORIGINAL BY SCHMUTZ-O-MATIC

LETTERCLOUD

WATERMELLONWORLD

CASH MONEY CARTOONS

G. W. DUNCANSON

XPLOTSIV PIZZA AND NECRONOMICOMIC &

DYLAN

TBD THE MOVIE POSTER

ZWIAN

THE WESTPORT MASSACRE AD

ZWIAN

EVERYTHING ELSE...

MR. SCRADAM

FIND THESE ARTISTS ONLINE

ZWIAN.TUMBLR.COM
WATERMELLONWORLD.TUMBLR.COM
TOM GARRETT - MRELLIOT.TUMBLR.COM
MIKEKRONBERGER.COM
SCHMUTZ-O-MATIC.TUMBLR.COM
KENAIM.TUMBLR.COM
HARRIS SMITH - NEGATIVEPLEASURE.TUMBLR.COM
ENCHANTEDCONSOLE.TUMBLR.COM
GW DUNCANSON - CASH-MONEY-CARTOONS.TUMBLR
SCRADAM.TUMBLR.COM